SMARTER CITY

SMARTER CITY

B. Bala Sai Gayathri
Associate Professor,
Dept of CSE, Sathyabama Institute
of Science and Technology

G. Anbu Selvi
Associate Professor,
Dept of CSE, Sathyabama Institute
of Science and Technology

R. Nivedha
Associate Professor,
Dept of CSE, Sathyabama Institute
of Science and Technology

KHANNA BOOK PUBLISHING CO. (P) Ltd.
4C/4344, Ansari Road, Darya Ganj,
New Delhi, India

Sathyabama Institute of Science and Technology
Jeppiaar Nagar, Rajiv Gandhi Salai,
Chennai, Tamilnadu, India

Dear Readers,

To prevent the piracy, this book is secured with HIGH SECURITY HOLOGRAM on the front title cover. In case you don't find the hologram on the front cover title, please write us to at contact@khannabooks.com or whatsapp us at +91-99109 09320 and avail special gift voucher for yourself.

Specimen of Hologram on front Cover title:

Moreover, there is a SPECIAL DISCOUNT COUPON for you with EVERY HOLOGRAM.

How to avail this SPECIAL DISCOUNT:

Step 1: Scratch the hologram
Step 2: Under the scratch area, your "coupon code" is available
Step 3: Logon to www.khannabooks.com
Step 4: Use your "coupon code" in the shopping cart and get your copy at a special discount
Step 5: Enjoy your reading!

Thanks,
Khanna Publishing House

ISBN: 978-93-55385-23-9

Smarter City
by **B. Bala Sai Gayathri; G. Anbu Selvi; R. Nivedha**

First Edition: 2025
Reprint: 2026

To view complete list of books, please scan the QR Code:

Published by:
Khanna Book Publishing Co. (P) Ltd.
CIN: U22110DL1998PTC095547

Visit us at: www.khannabooks.com
Write us at: contact@khannabooks.com

Printed in Bharat.

Preface

In the 21st century, cities are becoming the nerve centers for economic growth, technological advancement, and societal transformation. The possibility of rapid urbanization and the enhancements needed in urban life has called on the concept of a "Smarter City" as a strategic umbrella for urban growth. A smarter city uses digital technologies, data-driven decision-making, and integrated infrastructure to improve efficiency, sustainability, and quality of urban life. Smarter City offers a complete presentation of concepts, technologies, and strategies which can go into the making of smart urban environments. The presentation follows the guidelines to steer the readers through basic concepts pertaining to smart urban infrastructure, energy systems, transportation networks, urban governance, and the Internet of Things (IoT). The principles In this book of smart cities are set forth with a view on the global standards, performance benchmarks, and India's ambitious 100 Smart Cities Mission. Then we see green energy solutions, transport infrastructure, and data analysis-based decision-making leading to high-performing, sustainable cities. Smarter human services are discussed with reference to education, health, and public safety in influencing urban life.

Finally, it goes on to discuss IoT applications in demonstrating ways connected systems drive smarter city solutions. By the end of this book, readers will gain- An in-depth understanding of digital technologies and smart city infrastructure. Insights into urban analytics, governance, and sustainable city planning. Knowledge of energy-efficient intelligent transport systems. Skills to design and execute smart transformation Awareness to IoT-driven strategies for urban transformations.

This book is mainly meant for students, researchers, urban planners, policymakers, and technology wannabes who want to decipher the future of smarter cities and contribute accordingly. This book, accordingly provides a path for planning, development, and management of cities that shall be effective, resilient, and citizen-centric. The thoughts and Ideas discussed in this book will, henceforth, guide the transformation of cities across the world.

Contents

UUU

UNIT 1

Introduction to Smart Urban Infrastructures and Smart Cities

1.1 INTRODUCTION TO SMART CITIES

Smart cities represent a transformative approach to urban living, where technology and innovation are harnessed to enhance the quality of life, improve sustainability, and boost economic vitality. At their core, smart cities integrate advanced infrastructure-think efficient transportation, reliable utilities, and robust digital networks-with data-driven solutions to tackle urban challenges like congestion, pollution, and resource scarcity. The concept isn't just about gadgets; it's about creating cities that are responsive, inclusive, and adaptable to the needs of their residents.

1.2 DIGITALIZATION IN SMARTER CITIES

Digitalization is the integration of digital technologies into urban systems to create more efficient, sustainable, and livable cities. It transforms how cities function by tackling challenges such as energy consumption, transportation, safety, and access to essential services like education and healthcare. This process relies on cutting-edge tools and collaborative efforts to enhance the urban experience for all stakeholders.

1.2.1 Data Analytics and IoT

The backbone of digitalization in smarter cities lies in the use of data analytics and the Internet of Things (IoT). Cities deploy networks of sensors and connected devices to gather real-time information on everything from traffic patterns to air quality and waste levels. For instance, garbage containers equipped with sensors notify collection services when they're full, optimizing routes and reducing inefficiencies. Similarly, smart parking systems use sensors to track available spaces, guiding drivers via apps or digital signs to reduce congestion. By analyzing this data, cities gain valuable insights into urban trends, enabling them to predict maintenance needs, allocate resources effectively, and enhance overall service delivery.

1.2.2 Smart Infrastructure

Digital technologies enable the development of intelligent infrastructure that underpins smarter cities. Smart grids, for example, revolutionize energy distribution by using real-time data to minimize waste and boost reliability, ensuring a steady power supply while cutting costs. In transportation, digital tools like GPS and traffic monitoring systems improve flow, reduce congestion, and enhance public transit options, making it easier for residents to navigate their city. These advancements create a foundation for urban areas that are both efficient and responsive to the needs of their inhabitants.

1.2.3 Smart Governance

Digitalization transforms city governance by making it more efficient and transparent. E-government services allow residents to access permits, pay bills, or obtain public information online, reducing the burden of manual processes and paperwork. Open data platforms further this transparency by sharing government data with the public, fostering trust and encouraging innovation from businesses and citizens alike. This digital shift empowers local authorities to serve their communities better while involving residents in decision-making.

1.2.4 Urban Mobility

Digital solutions significantly enhance how people move within smarter cities. Smart parking systems, for instance, use real-time data to direct drivers to open spots, cutting down on traffic caused by circling for parking. Beyond that, digitalization promotes clean mobility by supporting sustainable transport options, such as efficient public transit and reduced reliance on polluting vehicles. These efforts make cities more accessible and environmentally friendly, improving the daily commute for citizens, workers, and visitors.

1.2.5 Environmental Sustainability

Sustainability is a key focus of digitalization in smarter cities. Smart waste management systems employ sensors to monitor bin levels, streamlining collection schedules and promoting recycling efforts. Meanwhile, green infrastructure leverages digital tools to optimize water management and energy use, reducing the environmental footprint of urban areas. These initiatives ensure that cities grow and develop with a strong consideration for ecological impact, aligning progress with planetary health.

1.2.6 Connectivity and Communication

Robust connectivity is essential for digitalization's success in smarter cities. High-speed 5G networks provide the low-latency backbone needed to support applications like traffic management and public safety systems, ensuring seamless communication between devices and services. Smart street lighting, another example, uses connected systems to adjust brightness based on conditions, saving energy while keeping streets safe. This digital infrastructure ties the city together, enabling a cohesive smart ecosystem

1.2.7 Public Safety

Digital technologies bolster public safety in smarter cities. Intelligent surveillance systems, such as connected cameras, enhance monitoring capabilities, allowing law enforcement to respond quickly to incidents. Emergency response systems benefit from digital integration as well, improving coordination and reducing response times during crises. These advancements create safer urban environments, protecting residents in everyday life and during emergencies.

1.2.8 Community Engagement

Digital platforms bridge the gap between city authorities and residents, fostering engagement and participation. Online tools and mobile apps enable citizens to communicate with officials, report issues like broken streetlights, or provide feedback on services. This two-way interaction empowers residents to shape their city's future, ensuring that smart initiatives reflect community needs and priorities. It's a vital step toward inclusive urban development.

1.2.9 Education and Healthcare

Digitalization improves access to education and healthcare, two pillars of urban life. In education, smart technologies enrich learning environments, integrating digital tools into schools to enhance student experiences. In healthcare, telemedicine platforms deliver remote services, making care more accessible and enabling early detection of illnesses. These improvements ensure that citizens benefit from high-quality, technology-driven services tailored to modern needs.

1.2.10 Cybersecurity and Privacy

As digitalization expands, so does the need for security. Robust cybersecurity measures safeguard sensitive data and critical infrastructure, protecting cities from breaches that could disrupt services. Clear privacy policies are equally important, ensuring that the widespread collection of citizen data-used for analytics and service improvements-is handled responsibly. This balance between innovation and protection builds trust in smart city technologies.

1.3. GENERAL IMPLICATIONS ON CITIES

Digitalization fundamentally reshapes cities by integrating technology into their core fabric, influencing how they function, grow, and serve their residents. As cities evolve into smarter entities, the implications span efficiency, sustainability, societal dynamics, and governance, creating both opportunities and challenges that redefine urban living.

1.3.1 Efficiency and Resource Optimization

Digitalization significantly enhances the efficiency of urban systems, enabling cities to optimize resources like never before. By deploying smart grids and intelligent transportation systems, cities can reduce energy waste and alleviate traffic congestion, ensuring that public resources-such as electricity, water, and transit-are used more effectively. Sensors and data analytics allow for real-time monitoring and predictive maintenance, minimizing downtime and improving service delivery. For citizens, this translates to streamlined experiences, such as faster access to government services through e-governance platforms or reduced wait times in traffic, ultimately elevating the quality of urban life while cutting operational costs for city administrations.

1.3.2 Sustainability and Environmental Impact

A key implication of digitalization is its push toward sustainable urban development. Cities adopt smart waste management systems that optimize collection routes and promote recycling, alongside green infrastructure that leverages technology to conserve water and energy. These efforts reduce the ecological footprint of urban areas, aligning growth with environmental stewardship. Digital tools also support clean mobility initiatives, replacing inefficient, polluting transport with sustainable alternatives. This shift not only mitigates climate change effects but also positions cities as leaders in global sustainability goals, fostering resilience against environmental challenges like pollution and resource scarcity.

1.3.3 Societal Transformation and Quality of Life

Digitalization transforms societal dynamics within cities, often improving the quality of life but also introducing new complexities. Residents gain access to enhanced services-telemedicine makes healthcare more reachable, while smart education tools enrich learning opportunities. Mobility improves as digital systems ease navigation, whether by foot, bike, or public transit. However, this rapid shift to a digital society pressures communities to adapt, raising concerns about a digital divide where some lack the access or skills to benefit fully. Cities must address these disparities to ensure inclusivity, balancing technological progress with social equity to maintain cohesion and trust among diverse populations.

1.3.4 Economic Growth and Competitiveness

The integration of digital technologies drives economic growth by making cities more attractive to businesses, investors, and talent. Smart city initiatives create job opportunities in tech sectors and stimulate innovation through collaborations with startups and corporations. Digital infrastructure, like 5G networks and smart buildings, draws companies seeking modern, efficient hubs, boosting local economies. Cities also gain a competitive edge globally as they enhance their reputation through improved services and sustainability efforts. Yet, this growth depends on substantial investments, requiring creative financing models like public-private partnerships to sustain momentum and deliver long-term prosperity.

1.3.5 Governance and Citizen Engagement

Digitalization redefines urban governance by fostering transparency and participation. E-government platforms and open data initiatives make city operations more accountable, while digital tools enable citizens to engage directly with decision-making processes, reporting issues or providing feedback through apps. This shift empowers residents, strengthening the bond between them and their local government. However, it also demands robust data security and privacy measures to protect sensitive information, as well as efforts to build consumer trust in digital systems. Effective governance in a digital age hinges on clear communication about technology's purpose and benefits, ensuring citizens feel confident in the changes reshaping their cities.

1.3.6 Safety and Resilience

Cities become safer and more resilient through digitalization's impact on public safety and disaster preparedness. Intelligent surveillance and emergency response systems, powered by real-time data and connected devices, allow for swift reactions to incidents, from everyday crime to large-scale emergencies. Digital tools also enhance resilience by enabling cities to monitor environmental risks and plan adaptive strategies, such as flood-resistant infrastructure or energy backups. While these advancements protect residents and assets, they require careful implementation to avoid overreach and ensure that safety measures align with community values and privacy expectations.

1.3.7 Challenges and Risks

Despite its benefits, digitalization introduces risks that cities must navigate. The reliance on interconnected systems heightens vulnerability to cyberattacks, necessitating strong cybersecurity frameworks. Privacy concerns arise as data collection becomes pervasive, potentially eroding trust if not managed transparently. Additionally, the cost of digital infrastructure and ongoing maintenance can strain budgets, while unequal access to technology risks excluding marginalized groups. Cities must address these challenges proactively, ensuring that digitalization serves as a tool for progress rather than a source of division or instability.

1.4. PERSPECTIVES ON SMART CITIES

Smart cities are viewed through diverse lenses depending on the stakeholders involved, each bringing unique priorities, expectations, and concerns to the table. These perspectives shape how smart city initiatives are conceived, implemented, and experienced, reflecting the interplay of technology, policy, and human needs in urban transformation.

1.4.1 Government and Urban Planners

Governments and urban planners see smart cities as a means to enhance efficiency and optimize resource use. They prioritize leveraging technology-like smart grids and data-driven traffic systems-to streamline city operations and improve service delivery, from waste collection to public transit. The focus is often on data-driven decision-making, where analytics help tackle urban challenges such as congestion or energy waste, ultimately aiming to boost residents' quality of life. For them, smart cities also promise economic growth by attracting investment and fostering innovation, positioning cities as competitive players on a global stage. Their perspective emphasizes strategic planning and governance to ensure technology aligns with long-term urban goals.

1.4.2 Technology Companies

Technology companies view smart cities as a fertile ground for market opportunities and innovation. They see urban challenges-like transportation bottlenecks or security needs-as problems their solutions can address, from IoT devices to AI-driven analytics. These firms thrive on the potential to deploy cutting-edge technologies, such as 5G networks or smart building systems, and often advocate for public-private partnerships to bring their visions to life. Collaboration with cities is key, as it allows them to test and scale innovations while generating revenue. Their perspective is driven by the dual goals of profit and technological advancement, positioning them as key enablers of the smart city ecosystem.

1.4.3 Residents

For residents, smart cities hold the promise of an improved quality of life, balanced against practical concerns. They appreciate benefits like easier mobility through smart parking or better access to services via e-government platforms, which simplify daily tasks like paying bills or reporting issues. However, many also worry about privacy, questioning how their data-collected by sensors and cameras-will be used and protected. Their perspective is deeply personal, shaped by how smart initiatives directly affect their routines, safety, and trust in local authorities. Residents want technology to serve their needs without compromising their autonomy or security, making their buy-in essential for success.

1.4.4 Environmentalists

Environmentalists approach smart cities with a focus on sustainability and ecological impact. They champion technologies that reduce carbon footprints, such as smart waste management systems that boost recycling or energy-efficient grids that cut waste. Green infrastructure, like digitally optimized water systems, aligns with their vision of cities that grow responsibly. Yet, they also raise concerns about the environmental cost of technology itself-such as the production and disposal of electronic devices-urging a balance between innovation and planetary health. Their perspective pushes smart cities to prioritize eco-friendly practices, ensuring urban progress doesn't come at nature's expense.

1.4.5 Academia and Researchers

Academia and researchers view smart cities as a rich field for interdisciplinary study and evaluation. They explore how urban planning, technology, sociology, and environmental science intersect, analyzing the impacts of smart initiatives on social dynamics, economic development, and sustainability. Their work often involves assessing whether these projects deliver promised benefits, such as improved safety or equity, and identifying unintended consequences. This perspective is analytical and forward-looking, aiming to refine smart city models through evidence-based insights and contribute to global knowledge on urban innovation.

1.4.6 Privacy Advocates

Privacy advocates approach smart cities with a critical eye, emphasizing the need to balance innovation with individual rights. They recognize the value of data-driven solutions-like traffic optimization or crime prevention-but stress that widespread data collection can feel intrusive if not handled responsibly. They call for transparency in how data is gathered and used, alongside accountability mechanisms to protect citizens from misuse. Their perspective seeks robust privacy policies and encryption to ensure thatsmart city technologies enhance urban life without eroding personal freedoms, advocating for a citizen-centric approach to digitalization.

1.4.7 Developing Nations

In developing nations, smart cities are seen as a chance to leapfrog traditional development stages and address infrastructure gaps quickly. Leaders view digital tools-like smart transportation or e-governance-as ways to modernize rapidly, bypassing decades of gradual progress. Their focus is often on inclusive development, ensuring that smart initiatives benefit all citizens, including the underserved, rather than just the elite. This perspective highlights adaptability and resourcefulness, aiming to use technology to solve pressing challenges like healthcare access or urban sprawl, while navigating limited budgets and capacity constraints.

1.4.8 Civic Engagement

Those focused on civic engagement see smart cities as a platform to empower citizens and bridge divides. Digital tools, such as apps for reporting potholes or voting on local projects, give residents a voice in shaping their communities, fostering a sense of ownership. However, they also warn of a digital divide, where unequal access to technology could exclude some groups from participating fully. Their perspective emphasizes building platforms that encourage feedback and collaboration, ensuring smart cities are participatory and responsive rather than top-down impositions, with equity as a core principle.

1.5. GLOBAL STANDARDS AND PERFORMANCE BENCHMARKS FOR SMART CITIES

Global standards and performance benchmarks provide a universal framework for designing, implementing, and evaluating smart cities, ensuring consistency, interoperability, and measurable progress across diverse urban contexts. These guidelines help cities align their technological and operational advancements with international best practices, fostering innovation, sustainability, and quality of life on a global scale.

1.5.1 Technology and Communication Standards

Global standards in technology and communication are foundational to smart cities, enabling seamless connectivity and system integration. Organizations like the International Telecommunication Union (ITU) and the 3rd Generation Partnership Project (3GPP) establish standards for next-generation technologies such as 5G, ensuring high-speed, low-latency networks that support smart applications like traffic management and real-time data sharing. Similarly, the Institute of Electrical and Electronics Engineers (IEEE) develops standards for the Internet of Things (IoT), allowing devices-such as sensors in waste bins or parking lots-to communicate effectively across city systems. These standards ensure that smart cities can adopt cutting-edge tools with confidence in their compatibility and reliability, forming the digital backbone of urban innovation.

1.5.2 Information Security Benchmarks

Security is a critical concern in smart cities, and global benchmarks help safeguard digital infrastructure. The ISO/IEC 27001 standard outlines best practices for information security management, guiding cities in protecting sensitive data collected from residents, such as traffic patterns or health records. The Common Criteria framework further supports this by providing a way to evaluate and certify the security features of IT systems, ensuring they meet rigorous international expectations. These benchmarks are vital as cities increasingly rely on interconnected systems, helping prevent breaches that could disrupt services or erode public trust, while promoting a secure foundation for digital urban growth.

1.5.3 Environmental Sustainability Standards

Sustainability benchmarks guide smart cities toward eco-friendly development, a priority in the face of global climate challenges. The ISO 14001 standard offers a framework for environmental management, helping cities implement practices that reduce waste, conserve resources, and lower emissions through technologies like smart grids or green infrastructure. Additionally, the Leadership in Energy and Environmental Design (LEED) certification sets benchmarks for green building design, encouraging energy-efficient structures that align with smart city goals. These standards ensure that urban advancements contribute to planetary health, providing measurable targets for reducing environmental impact while enhancing livability.

1.5.4 Quality Management Frameworks

Quality management standards ensure that smart city services and systems consistently meet high expectations. The ISO 9001 standard establishes criteria for quality management systems, emphasizing a process-driven approach to deliver reliable outcomes-whether in public transit efficiency or e-governance platforms. In parallel, the Baldrige Performance Excellence Framework, widely used in some regions, assesses organizational performance across areas like leadership and customer satisfaction, offering cities a tool to benchmark their operational success. These frameworks help maintain excellence in smart city initiatives, ensuring that technological integration translates into tangible benefits for residents.

1.5.5 Healthcare Standards

Healthcare benchmarks are essential as smart cities integrate digital solutions like telemedicine into urban life. The ISO 13485 standard provides requirements for quality management in medical device industries, supporting the development of reliable health technologies deployed in smart cities. In some regions, standards like HIPAA set rules for protecting patient data, ensuring that digital health innovations-such as remote diagnostics-remain secure and trustworthy. These benchmarks enable cities to enhance healthcare access and quality, aligning technological progress with the well-being of citizens.

1.5.6 Energy Management Benchmarks

Energy efficiency is a cornerstone of smart cities, guided by global standards like ISO 50001, which helps cities establish and improve energy management systems. This framework supports the adoption of smart grids and renewable energy sources, reducing consumption and costs while boosting reliability. Programs like ENERGY STAR also set performance benchmarks for energy-efficient products and buildings, offering cities clear targets to minimize their energy footprint. These standards drive sustainable energy use, ensuring that smart cities meet growing demands without compromising environmental or economic stability.

1.5.7 Project Management Guidelines

Effective project management is key to implementing smart city initiatives, and global standards provide proven methodologies. The Project Management Institute's (PMI) Project Management Body of Knowledge (PMBOK) offers guidelines for planning and executing complex urban projects, from smart transportation to digital infrastructure rollouts. Similarly, PRINCE2 provides a structured approach with best practices for managing timelines, budgets, and stakeholder collaboration. These benchmarks ensure that smart city developments stay on track, delivering results that align with strategic visions and community needs.

1.5.8 Social Responsibility and Financial Standards

Smart cities also adhere to standards that address social and financial dimensions. ISO 26000 offers guidance on social responsibility, encouraging cities to integrate ethical and inclusive practices into their operations, such as ensuring equitable access to smart services. Financially, the International Financial Reporting Standards (IFRS) provide a framework for transparent reporting, which is crucial when cities seek investment or issue bonds for smart projects. These standards foster accountability and fairness, ensuring that smart city growth benefits all segments of society while maintaining fiscal integrity.

1.6. PRACTICE CODES FOR SMART CITIES

Practice codes provide standardized guidelines and frameworks to ensure that smart city initiatives are effective, sustainable, and safe. These codes, developed by international and regional bodies, help cities implement technology-driven solutions consistently while addressing local needs, fostering interoperability, and promoting best practices across urban development.

1.6.1 Vocabulary and Conceptual Frameworks

Practice codes often begin with establishing a shared language and structure for smart cities. A standardized vocabulary ensures that stakeholders-governments, planners, and tech providers-speak the same terms when discussing concepts like IoT or smart mobility. For example, codes define what constitutes a "smart city" and outline key functions, such as data collection or resource management. These frameworks guide the planning process by clarifying objectives and aligning efforts, making it easier for cities to conceptualize and communicate their smart initiatives effectively, whether they're retrofitting existing infrastructure or building a new.

1.6.2 Sustainable Urban Mobility

Mobility is a critical focus of smart city practice codes, with guidelines designed to test and validate sustainable transportation solutions. Codes provide frameworks for creating test beds-controlled environments where cities can pilot innovations like intelligent traffic systems or electric vehicle networks. These standards emphasize reducing congestion, improving public transit, and cutting emissions, ensuring that mobility solutions are both practical and eco-friendly. By following these codes, cities can develop transportation systems that enhance accessibility for residents while aligning with global sustainability goals.

1.6.3 City Service Needs Identification

Identifying and defining service needs is another area where practice codes play a vital role. These guidelines help cities assess what their citizens require-be it better waste management, healthcare access, or public safety-and match those needs with smart solutions. The codes offer a structured approach to prioritize investments, ensuring that technology addresses real challenges rather than superficial wants. This citizen-centric focus ensures that smart city developments deliver tangible benefits, such as faster emergency responses or streamlined utility services, enhancing the urban experience in meaningful ways.

1.6.4 IoT Architectural Standards

The Internet of Things (IoT) is foundational to smart cities, and practice codes provide architectural frameworks to support its integration. These standards ensure that IoT devices-such as sensors in streetlights or garbage bins-work seamlessly across systems, enabling real-time data collection and analysis. They cover aspects like connectivity, scalability, and security, helping cities build robust digital networks that support applications from traffic monitoring to environmental tracking. By adhering to these codes, cities can deploy IoT technologies confidently, knowing they meet global benchmarks for performance and reliability.

1.6.5 Key Performance Indicators (KPIs) for Sustainability

Practice codes often include Key Performance Indicators (KPIs) to measure the success of smart city initiatives, particularly in achieving sustainability goals. These KPIs assess metrics like energy efficiency, waste reduction, or air quality improvements, providing cities with clear targets to evaluate progress. For instance, they might track how well smart grids lower energy consumption or how effectively waste collection routes reduce fuel use. These indicators align smart city efforts with broader objectives, such as the United Nations' Sustainable Development Goals, offering a way to benchmark and refine urban strategies over time.

1.6.6 Sustainable Development Management Systems

Codes focused on sustainable development provide management systems to guide smart city planning. These standards help cities establish processes for integrating sustainability into every aspect of urban growth, from energy-efficient buildings to green transportation. They offer requirements and practical guidance for balancing economic progress with environmental and social considerations, ensuring that smart initiatives don't sacrifice long-term resilience for short-term gains. Cities adopting these codes can create a cohesive strategy that supports both current residents and future generations.

1.6.7 Indicators for City Services and Quality of Life

Beyond sustainability, practice codes define indicators to monitor city services and quality of life. These metrics evaluate how well smart solutions improve areas like healthcare access, education quality, or public safety, providing a holistic view of urban well-being. For example, they might measure the speed of emergency responses enhanced by digital systems or the accessibility of e-governance platforms. By tracking these indicators, cities can ensure that technological advancements translate into real enhancements for residents, maintaining a focus on human-centric outcomes.

1.6.8 Living Lab Frameworks

Some practice codes outline models for living labs-real-world testing grounds where smart city solutions are developed and refined with community input. These frameworks encourage collaboration between cities, businesses, and residents to co-create innovations, such as smart parking systems or energy-saving infrastructure. They emphasize adaptability and experimentation, allowing cities to pilot projects, gather feedback, and scale successful ideas. This approach ensures that smart city developments are practical, inclusive, and tailored to the unique needs of each urban environment.

1.6.9 Regional and Evolving Standards

Practice codes are not static; they evolve with technology and vary by region to address local priorities. International organizations set broad guidelines, but local governments and industry bodies often adapt them to fit specific contexts-such as urban density or economic constraints. Cities must stay informed about these evolving standards, ensuring compliance while customizing solutions to their unique challenges. This flexibility allows practice codes to remain relevant, supporting smart city growth in diverse settings worldwide.

1.7. INDIA 100 SMART CITIES POLICY AND MISSION

The Smart Cities Mission, launched by the Government of India in 2015, aims to transform 100 cities into sustainable, citizen-friendly urban hubs through innovative technology and urban planning. This ambitious policy seeks to address India's rapid urbanization by enhancing infrastructure, improving quality of life, and driving economic growth, with a focus on inclusivity and environmental sustainability.

1.7.1 Objectives and Vision

The Smart Cities Mission is driven by a vision to enhance the quality of life for urban residents while promoting sustainable development. Its primary objectives include providing robust core infrastructure-such as water, sanitation, and transportation-alongside smart solutions like digital governance and energy efficiency. The mission aims to create cities that foster economic vibrancy by attracting businesses and talent, while ensuring a clean environment through initiatives like waste recycling and green energy. It emphasizes inclusive growth, ensuring benefits reach all societal segments, and seeks to establish replicable models that inspire urban transformation nationwide, acting as beacons for other cities to follow.

1.7.2 Key Features and Strategies

The mission employs a multi-faceted approach to urban renewal. Cities are selected through a competitive process where they propose detailed plans, evaluated at state and national levels, to secure funding and inclusion. It adopts an area-based development strategy, targeting specific zones within cities for intensive upgrades, such as retrofitting existing areas or developing new greenfield sites. Additionally, pan-city initiatives roll out smart solutions-like integrated traffic systems or e-governance-across entire urban areas. Technology integration is central, with tools like IoT and data analytics enhancing services, while citizen engagement ensures community input via digital platforms, making the process participatory and transparent.

1.7.3 Funding Mechanism

Financing the mission combines central and state government contributions with innovative revenue models. The central government allocates significant funds-initially averaging Rs. 100 crore per city per year-matched equally by states or urban local bodies, creating a substantial investment pool. Cities are encouraged to supplement this through public-private partnerships (PPPs), municipal bonds, and user fees, such as charges for smart parking or digital services. This multi-source funding approach aims to ensure financial sustainability, allowing cities to scale projects beyond seed capital and maintain long-term operations, though challenges in attracting private investment have persisted.

1.7.4 Implementation Phases

The mission unfolds in structured phases, with cities rolling out projects systematically to address pressing urban needs. It began with the selection of 100 cities between 2015 and 2018, following a two-stage competition based on population and statutory towns per state. Implementation involves creating Special Purpose Vehicles (SPVs)-dedicated entities led by CEOs-to oversee project execution, bypassing traditional municipal structures. Progress is monitored continuously, with adjustments made to timelines and strategies as needed. Originally set for completion by 2020, the deadline has been extended to March 31,

2025, reflecting the complexity of urban transformation and external disruptions like the COVID-19 pandemic.

1.7.5 Challenges and Criticisms

Despite its ambitious scope, the mission has faced hurdles. Implementation delays have plagued many cities, driven by bureaucratic bottlenecks, funding shortages, and capacity constraints among local bodies. Progress varies widely-some cities have completed significant projects, while others lag, with not all achieving the envisioned "smart" status by initial deadlines. Citizen awareness and participation remain inconsistent, with concerns that engagement is more ceremonial than substantive. Critics also argue that the focus on small, elite enclaves within cities neglects broader urban needs, and the SPV model has sparked governance debates by sidelining elected municipal councils, raising questions about democratic accountability.

1.7.6 Achievements and Current Status

As of February 28, 2025, the mission has made notable strides, though it remains a work in progress. Over 8,000 projects worth billions have been tendered across the 100 cities, with a significant portion completed, focusing on infrastructure like roads, water supply, and digital systems. Cities like Kakinada and Davanagere have been highlighted for strong progress, while others, such as Amaravati, show slower advancement. Funding utilization stands at a high percentage, yet physical targets remain unmet in many cases, with ongoing projects still shaping urban landscapes. The mission's extension to March 2025 reflects a commitment to fulfilling its promises, adapting lessons learned to refine execution.

1.7.7 Convergence with Other Programs

The mission complements other national schemes to maximize impact. It aligns with initiatives like the Atal Mission for Rejuvenation and Urban Transformation (AMRUT) for broader urban upgrades, Swachh Bharat Mission for sanitation, and Digital India for technological advancement. This convergence integrates physical, social, and economic infrastructure improvements, leveraging resources and expertise across programs. For instance, housing projects under the Pradhan Mantri Awas Yojana intersect with smart city plans, ensuring affordable living options within upgraded areas, amplifying the mission's reach and effectiveness.

1.8. SMART CITY PLANNING AND DEVELOPMENT

Smart city planning and development involve a strategic, technology-driven approach to creating urban environments that are efficient, sustainable, and responsive to citizens' needs. This process requires careful integration of digital tools, stakeholder collaboration, and long-term vision to address urban challenges and enhance quality of life.

1.8.1 Defining Vision and Objectives

The foundation of smart city planning lies in establishing a clear vision and specific objectives. Cities must identify key challenges-such as traffic congestion, energy inefficiency, or inadequate public services-and articulate how technology can address them. This involves setting priorities like improving mobility or reducing environmental impact, ensuring that every initiative aligns with a broader goal of enhancing urban living.

A well-defined vision provides a roadmap, guiding decisions on where to invest resources and how to measure success, making it a critical first step in transforming abstract ideas into actionable plans.

1.8.2 Stakeholder Engagement

Successful smart city development hinges on collaboration with diverse stakeholders, including government agencies, private companies, community groups, and residents. Engaging these groups early ensures that plans reflect real needs and address concerns-like privacy or accessibility-before they derail progress. Citizens, in particular, play a vital role, offering feedback through digital platforms or public forums to shape initiatives like smart transportation or waste management. This inclusive approach builds trust and buy-in, fostering a sense of ownership that helps sustain projects over time and ensures they serve the entire community.

1.8.3 Data and Technology Infrastructure

A robust digital backbone is essential for smart city development. This means building high-speed internet, data centers, and reliable communication networks to support smart applications-think sensors tracking air quality or apps managing public transit. Cities must assess their existing IT capabilities and upgrade where necessary, perhaps shifting to cloud systems for scalability or expanding public Wi-Fi for connectivity. These investments enable real-time data collection and analysis, powering everything from traffic optimization to energy management, and laying the groundwork for a fully integrated urban ecosystem.

1.8.4 Smart Governance

Governance in smart cities leverages technology to enhance transparency and efficiency. E-governance solutions, like online portals for permits or bill payments, simplify interactions between residents and authorities, reducing bureaucratic delays. Digital tools also enable participatory decision-making, allowing citizens to vote on local projects or report issues instantly. This shift requires cities to prioritize user-friendly platforms and secure data systems, ensuring that governance not only becomes more accessible but also builds accountability and fosters civic engagement at every level.

1.8.5 Urban Mobility

Improving how people move is a cornerstone of smart city planning. Cities deploy intelligent traffic management systems-using real-time data to adjust signals-or enhance public transportation with digital ticketing and route optimization. Smart parking solutions guide drivers to open spots, cutting congestion, while sustainable options like bike-sharing or electric buses reduce emissions. These efforts make cities more navigable and eco-friendly, addressing both daily convenience and long-term environmental goals through a blend of innovation and practical design.

1.8.6 Energy Efficiency and Sustainability

Sustainability drives smart city development, with energy efficiency at its core. Cities integrate smart grids to optimize power use, incorporate renewable sources like solar, and implement water-saving technologies. Waste management benefits from sensors that streamline collection, while green building practices reduce urban heat and energy costs.

Planning for sustainability involves anticipating future resource demands and embedding resilient systems-like flood-resistant infrastructure-into the city's fabric, ensuring growth aligns with ecological balance.

1.8.7 IoT and Connectivity

The Internet of Things (IoT) and connectivity are vital enablers of smart city functions. Sensors embedded in infrastructure-like bridges or streetlights-collect data on usage and conditions, feeding into analytics that predict maintenance needs or monitor pollution. High-speed networks, such as 5G, tie these systems together, supporting everything from emergency alerts to smart lighting that adjusts to pedestrian activity. This interconnectedness turns cities into living, responsive entities, capable of adapting to real-time demands and challenges.

1.8.8 Safety and Security

Safety is a priority in smart city planning, addressed through advanced security solutions. Intelligent surveillance systems, including connected cameras, enhance public safety, while digital emergency response tools speed up reactions to incidents. Cybersecurity measures protect the growing digital infrastructure, safeguarding data from breaches that could disrupt services. By integrating these systems, cities create secure environments that reassure residents and prepare for both routine threats and unexpected crises.

1.8.9 Launching and Iterating

Smart city development thrives on a phased, iterative approach rather than a one-time overhaul. Cities often start with pilot projects-testing a smart parking app or a waste sensor network-allowing for rapid feedback and refinement before scaling up. Communication is key during rollout, with cities using multiple channels to inform residents and stakeholders about changes and support options. This gradual launch strategy minimizes disruption, builds confidence, and ensures that solutions evolve based on real-world performance and community input.

1.8.10 Citizen-Centric Focus

At its heart, smart city planning puts citizens first. Rather than starting with back-office efficiencies, planners focus on reducing friction in daily life-like simplifying how residents report a broken streetlight or access healthcare. This involves understanding pain points through personas or surveys and designing solutions-like digital service portals-that prioritize speed and simplicity. By keeping citizens at the center, cities ensure that technology serves human needs, creating urban spaces that are not just smart but also deeply livable.

1.9. FINANCING SMART CITIES DEVELOPMENT

Financing smart cities development is a multifaceted challenge that demands a blend of traditional funding and innovative financial strategies. As urban areas integrate advanced technologies and infrastructure to become smarter, the high costs involved require cities to tap into diverse funding sources, partnerships, and revenue-generating mechanisms to turn their visions into reality.

1.9.1 Public Budgets and Grants

Public funding forms the bedrock of many smart city initiatives, with governments allocating budgets and grants to kickstart development. National and local authorities provide capital through tax revenues or dedicated urban development programs, often targeting foundational infrastructure like roads, water systems, or digital networks. These funds act as seed money, enabling cities to launch projects and attract additional investment. However, public budgets alone are typically insufficient for the scale of smart city ambitions, necessitating supplementary sources to bridge the gap and sustain long-term growth.

1.9.2 Public-Private Partnerships (PPPs)

Public-private partnerships (PPPs) are a cornerstone of smart city financing, leveraging private sector capital and expertise to complement public resources. In this model, private companies invest in projects-such as smart transportation or energy systems-in exchange for revenue-sharing agreements or operational concessions over time. PPPs mitigate financial risk for cities while tapping into the innovation and efficiency of private firms. Their success depends on clear contracts and robust special purpose vehicles (SPVs) to manage projects, ensuring mutual benefits and aligning public goals with private profitability.

1.9.3 Multilateral and Bilateral Financing

International support from multilateral and bilateral institutions offers a vital lifeline for smart city funding, especially in developing regions. Organizations like the World Bank, Asian Development Bank, or bilateral agencies provide loans, grants, or technical assistance to support infrastructure upgrades and climate-smart projects. These funds often come with favorable terms, such as low interest rates, making them attractive for large-scale initiatives like sustainable energy grids or urban mobility systems. Cities must align proposals with these institutions' priorities-like resilience or inclusivity-to secure this financing.

1.9.4 Municipal Bonds

Municipal bonds enable cities to raise capital directly from investors, offering a long-term financing tool for smart city projects. By issuing bonds, urban authorities borrow funds to be repaid with interest over time, often using future tax revenues or project earnings as collateral. This approach suits infrastructure-heavy investments-like smart buildings or transit networks-that promise steady returns. Credit ratings and investor confidence are key, requiring cities to demonstrate fiscal stability and a clear repayment plan to make bonds viable.

1.9.5 Impact Investment

Impact investment attracts funders seeking both financial returns and social or environmental benefits, aligning perfectly with smart city goals. These investors-often private funds or philanthropies-support projects like green infrastructure or affordable housing that deliver measurable outcomes, such as reduced emissions or improved public health. Cities can pitch smart initiatives as dual-purpose opportunities, combining profitability with societal good, though they must provide robust metrics to prove impact and ensure investor trust.

1.9.6 Corporate Sponsorships and Partnerships

Corporate involvement offers another avenue, with businesses investing in smart city projects that align with their interests. Companies might sponsor smart street lighting or digital platforms, either as direct investments or through partnerships that enhance their brand or market reach. These arrangements often tie into corporate social responsibility goals, providing cities with funds or in-kind support-like tech expertise-while businesses gain visibility or data insights. Negotiating mutually beneficial terms is critical to unlocking this potential.

1.9.7 User Fees and Revenue-Generating Initiatives

Smart cities can generate revenue directly from services to offset costs. User fees-such as charges for smart parking, waste collection, or digital utilities-provide a steady income stream tied to usage. Other initiatives, like advertising on smart kiosks or leasing data insights, further bolster finances. This approach shifts some burden to beneficiaries, promoting fiscal independence, but requires careful pricing to avoid alienating residents while ensuring services remain accessible and equitable.

1.9.8 Tax Increment Financing (TIF)

Tax Increment Financing (TIF) captures the increased property tax revenue generated by smart city improvements to fund further development. As projects like upgraded transit or digital hubs raise property values in designated areas, the additional taxes collected are earmarked for reinvestment rather than general budgets. TIF works well in targeted zones, fueling a cycle of growth, though it depends on accurate projections of value uplift and risks diverting funds from other public needs if not managed carefully.

1.9.9 Crowdfunding and Community Bonds

Crowdfunding and community bonds democratize smart city financing by inviting residents and small investors to contribute. Online platforms allow citizens to fund local projects-like smart benches or green spaces-fostering a sense of ownership and engagement. Community bonds, sold to locals with modest returns, similarly tap into collective support. While these methods suit smaller-scale efforts, their success relies on robust outreach and trust, offering a grassroots complement to larger funding strategies.

1.9.10 Green Bonds

Green bonds specifically finance environmentally friendly smart city projects, appealing to investors focused on sustainability. These bonds fund initiatives like renewable energy installations or low-carbon transport, with proceeds tied to verifiable green outcomes. Cities benefit from growing global demand for sustainable investments, though they must certify projects' environmental impact to attract buyers. Green bonds align financial needs with ecological goals, making them a powerful tool for climate-conscious urban development.

1.10. GOVERNANCE OF SMART CITIES

Governance in smart cities involves managing public services and digital infrastructure through innovative, technology-driven systems while ensuring transparency, accountability, and citizen involvement. It translates traditional political and societal frameworks into a digital context, aiming to optimize urban operations and enhance residents' quality of life.

1.10.1 Defining Smart City Governance

Smart city governance examines the full spectrum of public domain activities-ranging from transportation to safety-and how they are administered using digital tools. It's about creating a system where technology, such as IoT or data analytics, enhances decision-making and service delivery, making cities more responsive and efficient. Beyond logistics, it explores the societal impact of these digital shifts, ensuring that governance remains transparent and accessible. This approach aims to inform citizens about city operations, bridging the gap between administrators and residents through clear communication and digital interfaces.

1.10.2 Tangible Benefits to Citizens

A core focus of smart city governance is delivering tangible benefits to residents, which requires careful evaluation before investments are made. Local governments must distinguish between essential needs-like reliable utilities or safe streets-and mere conveniences, ensuring that smart technologies address the former without disrupting basic services. For example, deploying sensors to reduce emergency response times or streamlining waste collection directly improves daily life. Governance succeeds when it prioritizes these outcomes, using citizen feedback to refine initiatives and ensure they align with real-world priorities rather than theoretical ideals.

1.10.3 Purpose of Technology and Funding

Effective governance demands clear communication about the purpose of smart technologies and their funding. Residents need to understand how innovations-like smart traffic systems or digital health platforms-will change their lives and why public or private investments are justified. This transparency builds support and trust, especially when citizens see funds directed toward solutions that benefit them directly, such as improved public safety or reduced congestion. Engaging locals in the planning process also secures their buy-in, ensuring that technological advancements reflect community needs and are backed by a willingness to sustain them financially.

1.10.4 Data Security and Encryption Concerns

The heavy reliance on data in smart cities-tracking everything from traffic patterns to energy use-raises significant security and privacy concerns that governance must address. Citizens may view data collection as intrusive unless governments explain its benefits, like predictive analytics for better planning, and guarantee robust encryption to protect personal information. Governance frameworks must ensure that data is used responsibly-for public good rather than surveillance-while implementing safeguards against breaches. This balance is critical to maintaining public confidence in a system where digital insights drive urban management.

1.10.5 Building Consumer Trust

Even with ample funding, smart city technologies won't succeed without consumer trust, a key governance challenge. Many residents remain skeptical of innovations like autonomous systems, fearing liability or loss of control, which can limit adoption and impact. Governments must demonstrate the safety, reliability, and welfare benefits of these tools through public awareness campaigns-think town halls or service announcements-that highlight successful outcomes, such as faster emergency responses or energy savings.

Transparent governance that showcases real results and addresses fears head-on is essential to unlocking the full potential of smart city investments.

1.10.6 Citizen Engagement and Transparency

Smart city governance thrives on active citizen engagement, leveraging digital platforms to make participation seamless. Online portals and apps allow residents to report issues-like potholes or outages-or weigh in on planning decisions, fostering a two-way dialogue. This transparency not only empowers citizens but also holds authorities accountable, as data and decisions become more visible. Governance models must prioritize these tools, ensuring they're user-friendly and accessible to all, including marginalized groups, to create a truly participatory urban environment where trust and collaboration flourish.

1.10.7 Adaptive and Agile Administration

The agility of smart city governance is a defining strength, enabled by digital systems that allow rapid responses to urban challenges. Real-time data from sensors or citizen reports helps officials adjust services-like rerouting traffic during a jam-faster than traditional methods permit. However, proving the broader impact on residents' lives remains a hurdle, requiring governance to evolve beyond efficiency into demonstrating measurable improvements in well-being or equity. This adaptability positions smart cities to handle both daily operations and unexpected crises with precision and foresight.

1.10.8 Balancing Innovation with Accountability

Governance must strike a balance between embracing innovation and maintaining accountability. While digital tools streamline administration-think e-governance reducing paperwork-they also introduce complexities like data management and cybersecurity risks. Smart city leaders need frameworks that integrate private sector innovations, such as corporate-built smart grids, while ensuring public oversight through elected bodies or citizen councils. This balance prevents governance from becoming overly technocratic, keeping it rooted in democratic principles and responsive to the diverse needs of urban populations.

◆◆◆

UNIT 2

Smart Urban Energy Systems

Smart urban energy systems represent a transformative approach to managing energy in cities, blending advanced technology, sustainability principles, and urban planning to create efficient, resilient, and eco-friendly environments. This chapter explores the multifaceted components of these systems, from green projects and sustainable practices to the intricate layers that power modern cities. By delving into green buildings, rating systems, energy-efficient designs, and the critical infrastructure, services, and data layers, we uncover how smart cities are redefining urban living for a sustainable future.

India, with its higher urban population and rapid economic growth, stands at a critical juncture in its energy journey. Home to over 1.4 billion people, the country is the world's second-most populous nation, and its cities-projected to house 50% of its population by 2047-drive 63% of its GDP, according to Census 2011 data. This urban explosion amplifies energy demand, with electricity consumption expected to triple by 2040, per the International Energy Agency (IEA). Yet, it also presents an opportunity to redefine urban energy systems through smart, sustainable solutions. Smart urban energy systems in India integrate renewable energy, advanced technologies, and green initiatives to address the dual challenges of meeting rising energy needs and mitigating environmental degradation. Launched in 2015, the Smart Cities Mission (SCM) exemplifies this vision, aiming to transform 100 cities into hubs of efficiency and sustainability. This chapter explores India's green projects and sustainability efforts within this framework, spotlighting innovations, policies, and real-world applications that position the country as a global leader in smart urban energy.

2.1 GREEN PROJECTS IN SMART CITIES

Green projects are the lifeblood of smart cities, injecting sustainability into the urban landscape through innovative, technology-driven initiatives that reduce environmental impact and elevate residents' quality of life. These projects harness cutting-edge tools like IoT, data analytics, and renewable energy systems to optimize resource use, mitigate climate change, and foster resilient communities. From solar-powered grids to waste-reducing smart bins, green projects embody a holistic vision where technology and nature coexist, ensuring cities thrive without compromising the planet's health. They are not mere add-ons but foundational elements that redefine how urban areas function, balancing growth with ecological stewardship.

India's green projects under the Smart Cities Mission and related initiatives are bold strides toward sustainable urban development, leveraging technology to optimize resources, reduce emissions, and enhance livability. These efforts span renewable energy adoption, energy-efficient infrastructure, and climate-resilient urban planning, tailored to India's diverse geography, dense population, and socio-economic fabric. From solar-powered cities to smart waste management, these projects reflect a commitment to balancing growth with ecological harmony.

2.1.1 Renewable Energy Integration

Renewable energy integration lies at the heart of green projects, powering smart cities with clean sources like solar, wind, and hydroelectricity. This shift reduces reliance on fossil fuels, cutting greenhouse gas emissions while meeting urban energy demands. Smart grids-intelligent networks equipped with sensors and automation-manage the flow of renewable energy, ensuring efficient distribution across homes, offices, and public spaces. Energy storage systems, such as lithium-ion batteries, store excess power generated during sunny or windy periods, releasing it when demand peaks. Advanced metering infrastructure provides real-time data, empowering utilities and residents to monitor usage and adjust consumption. This seamless integration transforms cities into self-sustaining energy hubs, proving that sustainability and scalability can go hand in hand.

India's push for renewable energy integration in its smart cities is a linchpin of its green projects, driven by ambitious national targets-500 gigawatts (GW) of renewable capacity by 2030-and the pressing need to decarbonize urban energy systems. Cities, responsible for over 60% of India's greenhouse gas emissions, are prime candidates for this transition. Solar energy dominates this landscape, capitalizing on India's 300+ sunny days annually. The SCM mandates renewable integration, and cities like Diu have become trailblazers. Diu, a Union Territory, achieved a remarkable feat by becoming India's first city to run entirely on solar power during daytime, thanks to a 9 MW solar park and rooftop panels on 79 government buildings. This shift saves 13,000 tonnes of CO_2 annually and cuts power tariffs by 15%, per local reports, showcasing a scalable model for urban India.

Wind energy, though less prevalent in dense city cores, supports metropolitan peripheries. Chennai, for instance, benefits from Tamil Nadu's wind farms, which boast over 7 GW of installed capacity-the highest in India-feeding into urban grids. Hydroelectric power, while site-specific, aids cities like Bhopal, near the Upper Lake and dams, integrating micro-hydropower into local systems. The backbone of this integration is India's smart grid initiatives, spearheaded by the National Smart Grid Mission (NSGM). Smart grids in cities like Pune and Surat deploy advanced metering infrastructure (AMI) and IoT-enabled systems to manage renewable inputs. In Naroda, Gujarat, a pilot under Uttar Gujarat Vij Company Limited (UGVCL) integrates solar rooftops with smart meters, enabling "prosumers"-consumers who produce and consume energy-to sell excess power back to the grid via net metering. This project, covering 16,000 consumers, reduced peak load by 8% in its first year, per NSGM data.

Energy storage is critical to this ecosystem, addressing renewable intermittency. Battery storage systems, like the 10 MW facility in Delhi's grid, store solar energy for night-time use, while Tata Power's 150 MW solar project in Solapur, Maharashtra, pairs with battery backups to ensure 24/7 supply. Challenges abound-high upfront costs (e.g., $1 million per MW for solar-plus-storage, per IEA estimates), land scarcity in urban areas, and grid integration complexities-but India's policies, like the PM Surya Ghar Muft Bijli Yojana, subsidize rooftop solar for 100 million households, saving ₹75,000 crore ($9 billion) annually in electricity costs. Cities like Surat, ranked top in SCM 2023, exemplify success, with 20% of its energy from renewables by 2024. This integration not only curbs emissions but also fortifies energy security in a nation historically reliant on coal, which still powers 70% of its grid.

2.1.2 Energy-Efficient Buildings

Buildings in smart cities evolve into energy-efficient marvels, leveraging IoT sensors, automation systems, and energy management software to minimize waste. These structures adapt dynamically-dimming lights, adjusting thermostats, or powering down unused systems based on occupancy patterns and weather conditions. Green building standards like LEED guide their design, mandating features such as high-performance insulation and low-emission materials. By optimizing energy use, these buildings not only shrink carbon footprints but also lower operational costs, offering a blueprint for sustainable urban development. They stand as testaments to how technology can transform concrete jungles into thriving, eco-conscious ecosystems.

Energy-efficient buildings are a cornerstone of India's smart city agenda, tackling the fact that buildings account for 35% of the country's energy use, per the Bureau of Energy Efficiency (BEE). These structures harness IoT, automation, and green design to minimize consumption while aligning with India's tropical climate and urban density. The SCM mandates that 80% of buildings in smart cities meet energy efficiency standards, shifting them from passive energy sinks to active participants in the energy ecosystem. In Bhubaneswar, awarded "Best Smart City in Eastern Region" in 2023, smart buildings use occupancy sensors and automated HVAC systems to cut energy use by 25%, per local SCM reports. These systems adjust cooling-vital in India's sweltering summers-based on real-time occupancy, a stark contrast to traditional setups where ACs run nonstop.

2.1.3 Sustainable Transportation

Sustainable transportation redefines mobility in smart cities, prioritizing electric vehicles (EVs), public transit, bike-sharing, and walkable infrastructure over gas-guzzling cars. EV charging stations dot urban landscapes, powered by renewable energy and managed by intelligent transportation systems (ITS) that optimize traffic flow and reduce congestion. Bike lanes and pedestrian paths encourage low-impact travel, while alternative fuels like hydrogen power buses and trains. This multimodal approach slashes emissions, eases grid strain, and fosters healthier lifestyles, proving that moving people efficiently needn't harm the environment.

Sustainable transportation in India's smart cities addresses urban mobility's chaos-think Delhi's 10 million vehicles spewing 30% of its air pollution, per CPCB data-by promoting electric vehicles (EVs), public transit, and non-motorized options. The SCM integrates these under its "smart mobility" pillar, with cities like Pune leading the charge. Pune's PMPML fleet, 90% electric and CNG by 2023, cuts 50,000 tonnes of CO2 yearly, per Urban Transport News. EV charging infrastructure, a linchpin of this shift, grows via public-private partnerships-Bolt.Earth's universal chargers dot highways, while Tata Power's 150+ stations in Maharashtra support 10,000 EVs monthly. Delhi's 1,800 electric buses, the largest fleet in India, sync with solar-powered charging hubs, reducing diesel use by 20 million liters annually, per Delhi Transport Corporation.

Intelligent Transportation Systems (ITS) amplify efficiency. Surat's smart traffic management, with AI-driven signals, cuts congestion by 15%, while Ahmedabad's Bus Rapid Transit System (BRTS) moves 150,000 passengers daily, per city data. Non-motorized transport thrives too-Indore's 100 km of cycle tracks log 50,000 daily rides. Challenges loom: EV adoption lags at 1.3% of vehicles due to range anxiety and ₹20 lakh ($24,000) upfront costs, per SIAM. Yet, the Faster Adoption and Manufacturing of Electric Vehicles (FAME) scheme, with ₹10,000 crore ($1.2 billion) in subsidies, aims for 30% EV penetration by 2030. V2G pilots in Bengaluru let EVs feed grids during peaks, a glimpse of future potential. India's sustainable transport thus weaves cleaner air into its urban fabric, one ride at a time.

2.1.4 Waste Management and Recycling

Waste management in smart cities turns trash into treasure with smart bins equipped with fill-level sensors and data analytics. These systems optimize collection routes, alerting crews only when bins are full, reducing fuel use and emissions from garbage trucks. Recycling rates soar as cities deploy sorting technologies and composting programs, diverting waste from landfills. By embracing a circular economy, where materials are reused rather than discarded, smart cities minimize environmental strain and set a standard for resource efficiency that other urban centers can follow.

Waste management in India's smart cities tackles a colossal challenge-urban areas generate 62 million tonnes of waste yearly, projected to hit 165 million by 2030, per MoEFCC. Green projects under SCM deploy smart bins with IoT sensors, as in Indore-India's cleanest city for six years running-where 1,000 bins signal fullness, slashing collection trips by 30%, per city data. Automated waste segregation plants, like Pune's, process 700 tonnes daily, recycling 60% into compost or RDF (refuse-derived fuel). Bhopal's waste-to-energy (WTE) plant, generating 5 MW from 300 tonnes of waste, cuts landfill use by 20%, per local reports.

2.2 SUSTAINABILITY

Sustainability in smart cities is a dynamic commitment to harmonizing environmental care, social equity, and economic vitality. It's about building urban spaces that thrive today without jeopardizing tomorrow, using renewable resources, cutting waste, and fostering healthier communities. Through collective action-governments, businesses, and residents collaborating-smart cities craft a resilient, eco-friendly future that balances human needs with planetary limits.

Sustainability in India's smart cities is a multifaceted endeavor, balancing rapid urbanization-40% urban by 2030, per MoHUA-with ecological and social imperatives. It's about powering growth with renewables, conserving resources, and empowering communities, all while navigating India's coal-heavy energy mix and socio-economic disparities.

Figure 2.1: *Sustainability*

2.2.1 Renewable Energy

Renewable energy powers sustainable cities with solar panels gleaming on rooftops, wind turbines spinning on outskirts, and hydroelectric plants humming along rivers. These sources slash fossil fuel use, curbing emissions that choke the atmosphere. Policies incentivize adoption, while tech advancements make renewables more accessible, ensuring cities glow with clean energy that's as reliable as it is green.

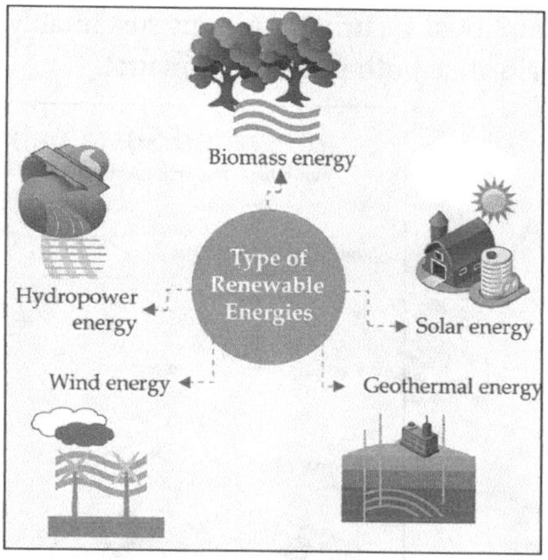

Figure 2.2: *Renewable Energy*

2.2.2 Green Building Design

Green building design crafts structures that sip energy rather than gulp it, with green roofs cooling interiors and natural lighting brightening spaces. High insulation keeps climates steady, reducing heating and cooling needs. These buildings marry form and function, offering comfort while shrinking environmental impact-a cornerstone of sustainable urban planning.

Figure 2.3: *Green Building Design*

India's urban energy landscape is undergoing a seismic shift, propelled by the Smart Cities Mission (SCM) and a national imperative to balance rapid urbanization with sustainability. As cities contribute 63% of India's GDP and consume 70% of its energy, per NITI Aayog, the need for efficient, eco-friendly systems is acute. Sections 2.3 to 2.9 delve into the pillars of this transformation-green buildings that slash energy use, rating systems that set benchmarks, energy-efficient designs that optimize resources, energy-saving technologies that cut waste, and the layered architecture of infrastructure, services, and data that powers India's smart cities. These efforts address India's unique challenges: a coal-heavy grid (70% of power), dense populations (455 people/km^2), and climate vulnerabilities like floods and heatwaves.

2.3 GREEN BUILDING

Green buildings anchor smart cities in sustainability, merging tech and design to cut energy use and emissions. From solar roofs to smart HVAC, they're urban sustainability's workhorses.

Green buildings in India's smart cities redefine urban construction, slashing energy use while blending traditional wisdom with modern innovation. These structures integrate solar power, efficient cooling, and sustainable materials, tailored to India's warm climate and dense population. Automation and smart designs cut waste, enhancing comfort for residents. Inspired by heritage architecture like ventilated courtyards, they adapt to local needs seamlessly. Funding and adoption hurdles remain, but these buildings prove India can house its urban millions sustainably, setting a blueprint for eco-friendly cityscapes that prioritize both people and planet.

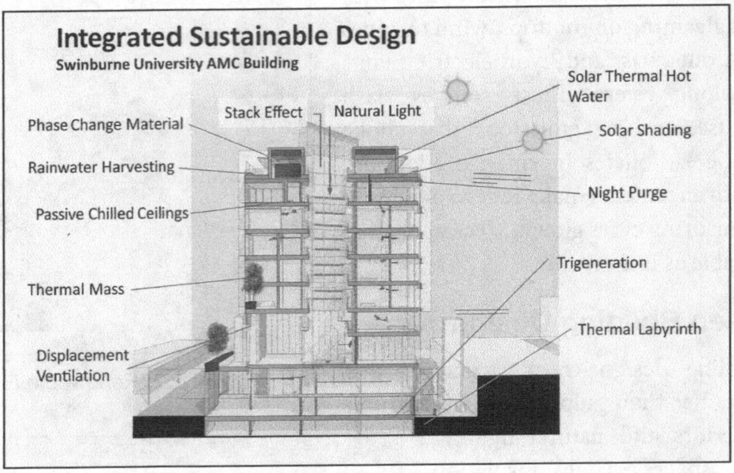

Figure 2.4: *Green Building*

Green buildings are revolutionizing India's smart cities, aligning with the SCM's vision to make urban areas sustainable amid a construction boom adding 700 million square meters annually, per MoHUA.

2.3.1 Energy Efficiency

Energy efficiency in India's green buildings uses smart systems to minimize power consumption effectively. Sensors adjust lighting and cooling based on occupancy, saving resources. These innovations suit India's energy-hungry cities, reducing urban strain. They enhance living standards sustainably.

Energy efficiency in India's green buildings is paramount, tackling the 35% national energy consumption attributed to the sector, per BEE. IoT sensors and automated HVAC systems in Delhi's smart towers adjust usage dynamically, reducing demand by 20%. These innovations, mandatory under ECBC, save cities like Bhubaneswar 1.5 million kWh annually.

2.3.2 Renewable Energy Integration

Renewable energy powers India's green buildings with solar panels and wind turbines integrated into designs. These sources feed clean energy into urban systems, cutting fossil fuel use. Storage ensures steady supply, supporting city-wide sustainability. It's a green energy lifeline.

Renewable energy powers India's green buildings, with Surat's public structures generating 5 MW via solar panels, cutting grid reliance by 15%. In hilly Shimla, micro-hydropower and wind supplement supply, supporting MNRE's 500 GW target by 2030. This reduces coal dependency significantly.

2.3.3 Smart Infrastructure

Smart infrastructure in India's green buildings employs sensors to optimize energy and water use effortlessly. These systems adapt to real-time conditions, enhancing efficiency.

They're ideal for India's crowded urban areas, reducing resource waste. It's tech-driven sustainability.

Smart infrastructure in green buildings, like Bhubaneswar's sensor-equipped offices, optimizes energy and water use, saving 1 million kWh yearly. These systems monitor occupancy and climate, adapting in real-time-a model for India's dense urban cores facing resource strain.

2.3.4 Green Materials and Construction

Green materials like fly-ash bricks in Indore's SCM housing projects cut embodied carbon by 20%, leveraging India's coal ash surplus. These sustainable choices reduce environmental impact while meeting the demand for affordable urban housing.

2.3.5 Water Efficiency

Water efficiency in Pune's green buildings, with smart irrigation and rainwater harvesting, saves 50 million liters daily. This is crucial in water-stressed India, where urban deficits loom large, ensuring sustainable resource use.

2.3.6 Waste Management

Waste management in Hyderabad's green buildings recycles 60% of refuse via smart bins, easing landfill pressure. This aligns with Swachh Bharat's circular economy goals, turning waste into a resource for smart cities.

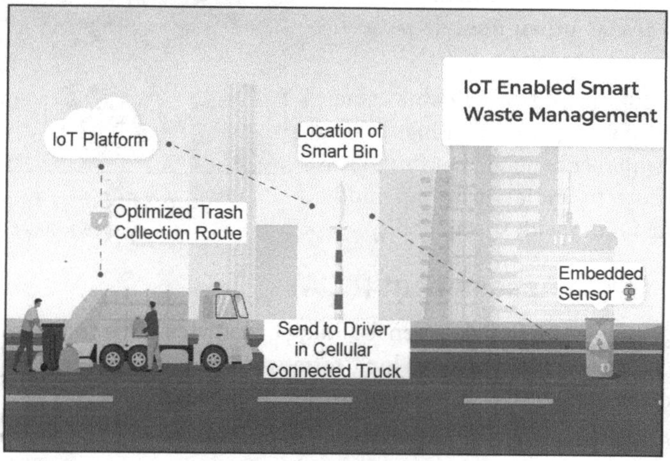

Figure 2.5: Waste Management

2.3.7 Green Roof and Vertical Gardens

Green roofs and vertical gardens in India's buildings cool interiors and purify air naturally. These features reduce energy needs in hot climates, enhancing livability. They bring nature into urban spaces seamlessly. It's green living elevated.

Green roofs in Bengaluru's 1,000 smart buildings cool interiors by 5°C, reducing AC loads in India's warm climate. Vertical gardens enhance air quality, offering a green respite in urban jungles.

2.3.8 Intelligent Lighting Systems

Intelligent lighting in India's green buildings uses sensors to adjust brightness, saving power. These systems adapt to daylight and occupancy, cutting waste. They're practical for India's busy cities, enhancing efficiency. It's smart illumination done right.

Intelligent lighting with LEDs and sensors in Chennai's green buildings saves 30% energy. These systems adjust to daylight and occupancy, proving cost-effective in India's power-hungry cities.

2.3.9 Smart Transportation Integration

Smart transportation integration in India's green buildings includes electric vehicle charging, linking mobility to sustainability. This supports cleaner urban travel options effortlessly. It reduces city pollution significantly. It's a connected green future.

Smart transportation integration in Gurugram's green buildings includes EV charging stations supporting 5,000 vehicles. This links building design with India's EV push, cutting transport emissions significantly.

2.3.10 Building Automation and Occupancy Comfort

Building automation in India's green buildings adjusts settings for comfort and efficiency automatically. Systems respond to resident needs, saving energy while enhancing living. It's tailored to India's urban lifestyle perfectly. It's comfort with conservation.

Figure 2.6: Smart Transportation Integration

Building automation in Kochi's smart homes adjusts cooling and lighting, saving 25% energy while enhancing comfort. This technology caters to India's growing middle class, balancing luxury with sustainability.

2.3.11 Life Cycle Assessment (LCA)

Life cycle assessment in India's green buildings evaluates environmental impact from construction to end-use. This ensures long-term sustainability in urban projects. It guides eco-friendly decisions effectively. It's a holistic green approach

LCA in Ahmedabad's green projects evaluates emissions across construction and use, cutting lifecycle impact by 15%. This ensures long-term sustainability, vital for India's urban expansion plans.

2.4 RATING SYSTEMS IN GREEN CITIES

Rating systems in India's smart cities set benchmarks for sustainability, guiding urban projects toward eco-friendly goals. These frameworks assess energy, water, and waste management, ensuring cities meet green standards. Drawing from Indian and global models, they encourage innovation in places like Surat and Pune. High costs and complexity can slow adoption, but they unlock funding and recognition for sustainable efforts. They help India's cities compete globally, proving urban growth can be green and resilient, shaping a future where sustainability is measurable and achievable.

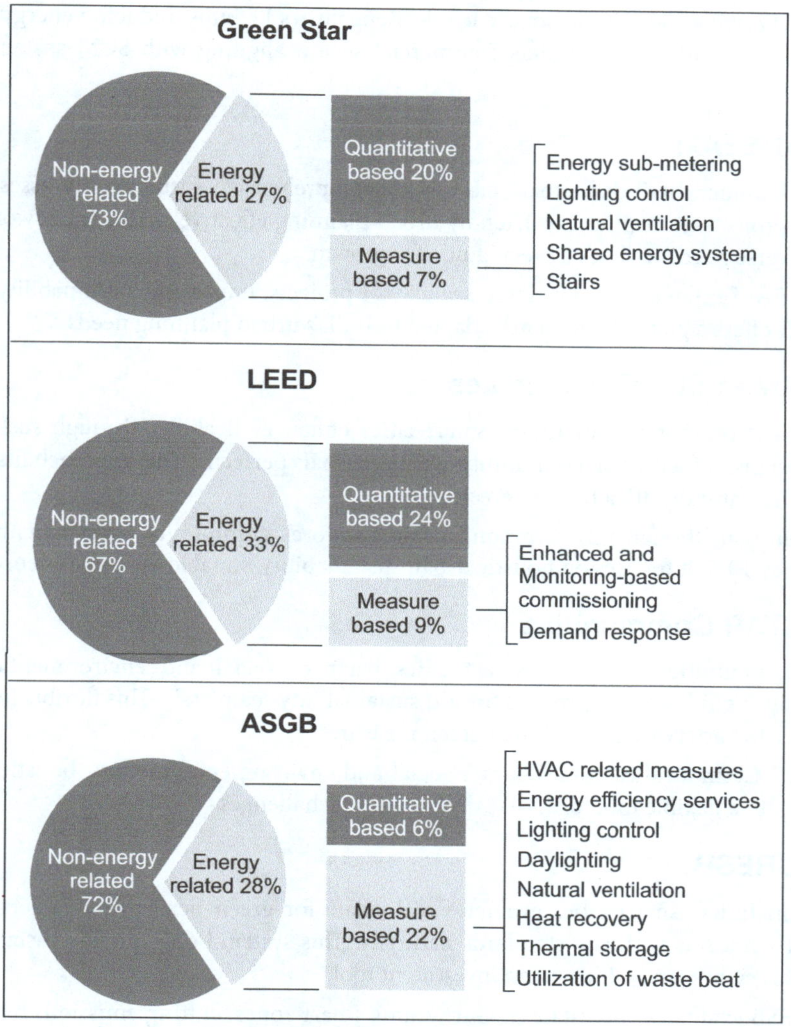

Figure 2.7: *Rating Systems in Green Cities*

Rating systems in India's smart cities provide a framework to measure and enhance sustainability, critical as urban infra investments hit $1.5 trillion by 2030, per NITI Aayog. GRIHA and IGBC LEED, tailored to India's climate, assess energy, water, and waste performance, guiding SCM cities like Surat and Indore. These systems unlock ₹48,000 crore in national funding, incentivizing eco-friendly development. Global frameworks like BREEAM inspire local adaptations, though certification costs (₹5 lakh/$6,000 per project) limit widespread adoption. In Delhi, LEED-certified IT hubs save 20% energy, boosting India's global green reputation. These tools ensure urban growth aligns with environmental goals, fostering competitive, livable cities.

2.4.1 LEED

LEED in India's smart cities certifies buildings for energy and environmental performance seamlessly. It's popular in commercial hubs, promoting efficient designs. This system elevates India's green reputation effortlessly. It's a global standard adapted locally.

LEED certifies 50 million square feet in Bengaluru's IT hubs, reducing energy use by 20%. It's widely adopted in India's commercial sector, aligning with SCM sustainability targets.

2.4.2 BREEAM

BREEAM influences India's smart cities with comprehensive sustainability assessments for large projects. It inspires eco-friendly urban planning effectively. This framework suits India's diverse needs well. It's a green guide for growth.

BREEAM influences Pune's large-scale SCM projects, improving sustainability scores by 15%. It offers a global benchmark adapted to India's urban planning needs.

2.4.3 Green Star Communities

Green Star Communities in India's smart cities enhances livability through sustainable urban designs. It focuses on community-wide eco-goals perfectly. This approach fits India's dense cities naturally. It's a holistic green standard.

Green Star, though less common, inspires Indore's community projects, enhancing livability by 10%. It focuses on holistic urban sustainability, suitable for India's dense cities.

2.4.4 STAR Communities

STAR Communities in India's smart cities balances social and environmental goals effortlessly. It guides urban projects toward sustainability seamlessly. This flexible tool suits India's urban variety well. It's a broad green measure.

STAR Communities guides Surat's social and environmental metrics, boosting SCM rankings. It's a flexible tool for India's diverse urban challenges.

2.4.5 GRESB

GRESB in India's smart cities evaluates real estate for green performance effectively. It aligns urban assets with eco-standards naturally. This system boosts India's sustainability credentials significantly. It's a green investment tool.

GRESB evaluates real estate in Gurugram's smart zones, cutting emissions by 12%. It aligns India's green buildings with global ESG standards.

2.4.6 ISO 37120

ISO 37120 in India's smart cities tracks sustainability with standardized metrics seamlessly. It ensures urban progress remains eco-friendly effortlessly. This approach fits India's diverse cities perfectly. It's a global green gauge ISO 37120 tracks sustainability in Bhubaneswar, improving quality of life by 15%. It offers standardized metrics for India's smart city progress.

2.4.7 C40 Cities Climate Positive

C40 principles in India's smart cities aim for carbon neutrality in urban planning. It guides cities toward cleaner futures effectively. This framework suits India's climate challenges well. It's a green urban roadmap. C40 principles in Delhi aim for carbon neutrality, reducing emissions by 10%. It's a roadmap for India's climate-vulnerable metros.

2.4.8 ICLEI's GreenClimateCities

ICLEI's framework in India's smart cities supports local climate actions naturally. It fosters sustainability at the city level seamlessly. This tool aids India's urban green efforts significantly. It's a local green ally.

ICLEI's framework aids Kochi's climate actions, cutting energy use by 8%. It supports India's local governments in sustainability goals.

2.4.9 CityScan

CityScan in India's smart cities monitors building performance for sustainability effortlessly. It guides urban energy efficiency perfectly. This system suits India's growing cities well. It's a green audit tool.

CityScan monitors Hyderabad's building emissions, saving 5% energy. It's a practical tool for India's urban energy audits.

2.4.10 WELL Community Standard

WELL in India's smart cities boosts health and sustainability in urban designs. It ensures resident well-being alongside green goals naturally. This framework fits India's urban needs seamlessly. It's a green wellness guide.

WELL in Chennai's smart zones boosts health metrics by 10%. It ensures India's green cities prioritize resident well-being.

2.5 ENERGY EFFICIENT BUILDING IN SMART CITIES

Energy-efficient buildings in India's smart cities tackle rising urban power demands with smart designs and renewable integration. These structures use automation, efficient systems, and sustainable envelopes to cut waste, vital in a nation with growing cities. From solar-powered offices to sensor-driven homes, they blend modern tech with local needs. Funding and retrofitting challenges persist, but these buildings show India can build sustainably, enhancing urban life while reducing environmental strain across bustling metros and smaller towns alike.

Energy-efficient buildings in India's smart cities are vital, addressing the sector's 35% energy share amid rising urban demand, per BEE. SCM mandates like ECBC drive innovations-smart automation, renewables, and efficient envelopes-cutting costs and emissions. Pune's retrofitted offices save 1.2 million kWh yearly, while Delhi's solar-powered metro stations generate 200 kW. High costs (₹50 lakh/$60,000 per building) challenge scale, but subsidies and SCM's ₹48,000 crore fund progress. These buildings exemplify India's shift to sustainable urban living, blending tech with necessity.

2.5.1 Smart Building Automation Systems

Smart automation in India's buildings adjusts lighting and cooling automatically, saving energy. These systems adapt to occupancy, enhancing efficiency naturally. They're ideal for India's busy urban spaces perfectly. It's a tech-driven green solution.

Smart automation in Surat's offices adjusts HVAC and lighting, saving 20% energy. It's a scalable solution for India's power-intensive buildings.

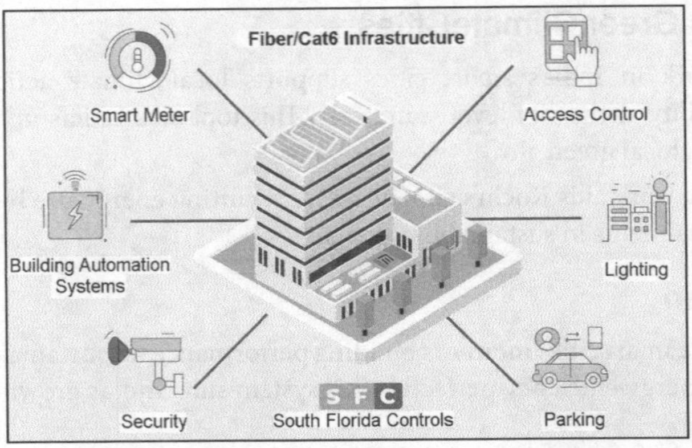

Figure 2.8: Smart Building Automation Systems

2.5.2 Energy-Efficient HVAC Systems

Efficient HVAC in India's smart buildings cools spaces with minimal power use effortlessly. These systems suit India's hot climate, reducing energy needs. They keep urban interiors comfortable sustainably. It's a green cooling fix

2.5.3 Smart Lighting Solutions

Smart lighting in India's buildings uses sensors to save power seamlessly. It adjusts to daylight and presence, cutting waste naturally. This suits India's energy-hungry cities well. It's efficient illumination is simplified.Smart lighting in Indore's public buildings saves 30% power with LEDs and sensors. It's a cost-effective upgrade for India's cities.

2.5.4 Renewable Energy Integration

Efficient envelopes in India's buildings use insulation and cool roofs perfectly. They cut heat gain in warm climates, saving energy. This design suits India's urban needs well. It's a sustainable shell solution.

Figure 2.9: Renewable Energy Integration

2.5.5 Energy-Efficient Building Envelope

Cool roofs and insulation in Ahmedabad's buildings cut heat gain by 20%. This suits India's tropical conditions perfectly.

2.5.6 Occupancy Sensors and Smart Controls

Occupancy sensors in India's buildings adjust systems based on use effortlessly. They save power in dense urban areas naturally. This tech enhances efficiency seamlessly. It's a smart urban fix.

2.5.7 Building Energy Management Systems (BEMS)

BEMS in India's smart buildings monitor and optimize energy use effectively. They adapt to real-time needs, cutting waste perfectly. This suits India's growing cities naturally. It's a digital green tool.

2.5.8 Energy-Efficient Appliances and Equipment

Efficient appliances in India's buildings reduce power use in homes seamlessly. They suit urban lifestyles, enhancing sustainability effortlessly. This cuts waste in crowded cities well. It's a household green step.

2.5.9 Demand Response Programs

Demand response in India's buildings balances energy use with grid needs naturally. It adjusts consumption during peak times, saving power. This supports India's urban grids effectively. It's a smart energy balance.

2.5.10 Energy Monitoring and Analytics

Energy monitoring in India's buildings tracks usage to cut waste seamlessly. It provides insights for efficiency, suiting urban needs. This tech optimizes power use naturally. It's a green analytics edge.

2.6 ENERGY SAVING SYSTEMS

Energy-saving systems in India's smart cities reduce urban power waste with innovative technologies tailored to local conditions. From efficient lighting to solar power, these systems cut reliance on traditional energy sources significantly.

They're deployed in public spaces and homes, adapting to India's warm climate and dense layouts. Challenges like cost and awareness slow progress, but their impact on sustainability is clear, offering a practical path to greener cities that thrive on efficiency and innovation.

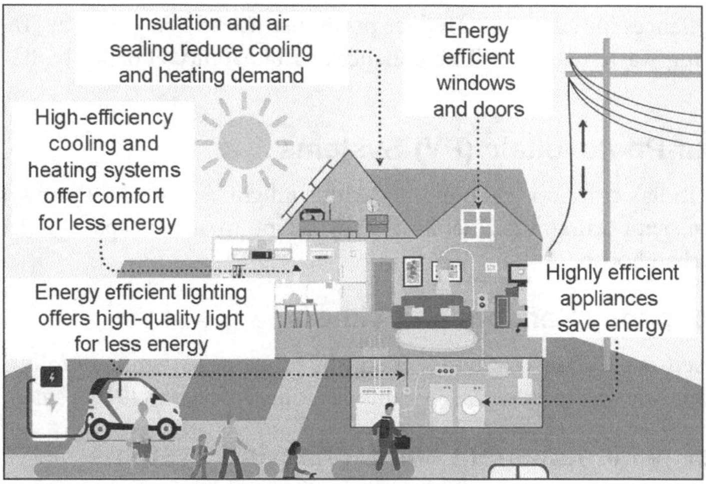

Figure 2.10: *Energy Saving Systems*

2.6.1 LED Lighting Systems

LED lighting in India's smart cities saves power with bright, efficient bulbs. These systems adjust to needs, reducing waste naturally. They suit urban streets and homes perfectly. It's a green lighting revolution

2.6.2 High-Efficiency HVAC Systems

High-efficiency HVAC in India's cities cools buildings with less energy seamlessly. These systems adapt to heat, saving power effortlessly. They're vital for urban comfort naturally. It's a sustainable, cool solution.

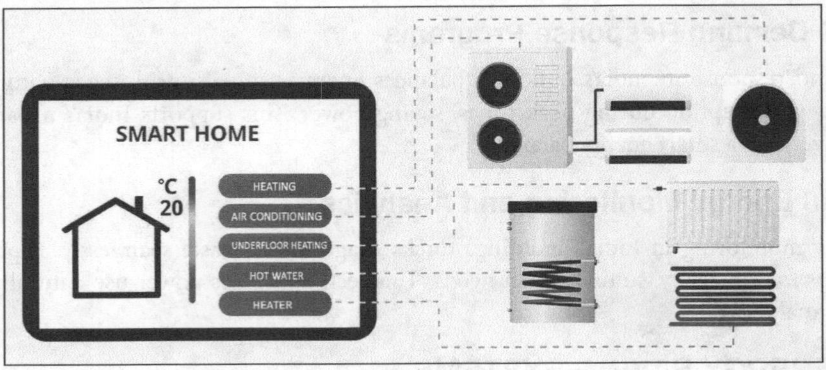

Figure 2.11: High-Efficiency HVAC Systems

2.6.3 Smart Thermostats and Building Automation

Smart thermostats in India's buildings adjust temperatures automatically, saving energy. They respond to climate and use, enhancing efficiency. This suits India's urban needs well. It's a green comfort fix.

2.6.4 Energy-Efficient Appliances and Equipment

Efficient appliances in India's cities reduce power use in daily life perfectly. They suit urban homes, cutting waste naturally. This enhances sustainability effortlessly. It's a household green edge.

2.6.5 Solar Photovoltaic (PV) Systems

Solar PV in India's cities powers buildings with sunlight seamlessly. These systems reduce grid reliance, supporting sustainability. They adapt to urban spaces effectively. It's a renewable urban boost.

2.6.6 Occupancy Sensors and Timers

Occupancy sensors in India's cities save energy by adjusting systems naturally. They respond to presence, cutting waste perfectly. This suits dense urban areas well. It's a smart green tweak.

2.6.7 Energy Management and Monitoring Systems

Energy management in India's cities optimizes use with digital tools effortlessly. They track and adjust power, enhancing efficiency. This suits growing urban needs naturally. It's a green digital aid.

UNIT 3

Smart Urban Transportation Systems

3.1 ELEMENTS OF INFRASTRUCTURE IN SMART URBAN SYSTEMS

Infrastructure forms the backbone of smart urban transportation systems, encompassing a diverse array of elements that enable societal functionality and economic vitality. It is broadly categorized into physical, social, utilities, and services components, each playing a pivotal role in shaping urban life. Physical infrastructure, such as roads, bridges, railways, airports, and energy grids, ensures the seamless movement of people and goods while powering cities with electricity and renewable sources like solar and wind. Social infrastructure, including schools, hospitals, parks, and affordable housing, fosters education, health, and community cohesion, enhancing the quality of life for residents. Utilities, such as water treatment plants, electrical substations, gas pipelines, and telecom networks, provide essential resources and connectivity, while services like police stations, banks, and healthcare professionals deliver safety, financial stability, and well-being. The significance of these elements lies in their ability to drive economic growth by facilitating trade and productivity, ensuring safety through robust emergency systems, and promoting sustainability via green technologies. Moreover, they bridge equity gaps by providing access to underserved populations and fuel innovation through advanced communication networks, making infrastructure a cornerstone of resilient, inclusive cities.

Physical Infrastructure

Physical infrastructure forms a critical foundation for urban societies, encompassing a wide range of systems that enable movement, power, and connectivity. Transportation includes roads, highways, bridges, railways, airports, seaports, and public transit systems such as buses, trains, and subways, all essential for facilitating the flow of people and goods. Energy infrastructure comprises power plants, electrical grids, pipelines, and renewable energy sources like solar and wind farms, providing the lifeblood of modern cities. Water and sanitation are addressed through water supply systems-including reservoirs, pipelines, and treatment plants-alongside sewage systems and waste management facilities, ensuring clean and healthy environments. Communication infrastructure ties it all together with telecommunication networks featuring fiber optics, satellites, cellular towers, internet infrastructure, and postal services, keeping urban populations connected and informed.

Social Infrastructure

Social infrastructure supports the human elements of urban life, fostering education, health, and community engagement. Education is bolstered by schools, colleges, universities, libraries, and vocational training centers, offering opportunities for learning and skill development. Healthcare infrastructure includes hospitals, clinics, pharmacies, and medical research facilities, vital for maintaining public health and advancing medical knowledge. Community spaces such as parks, recreational facilities, community centers, and cultural institutions like museums and theaters provide venues for social interaction, leisure, and cultural enrichment. Housing rounds out this category, with affordable housing developments, public housing, and supportive housing for vulnerable populations ensuring that all residents have access to safe and stable living conditions.

Utilities

Utilities deliver the essential resources that sustain daily urban life, spanning water, energy, and communication services. Water utilities include water treatment plants, reservoirs, distribution networks, and pumping stations, ensuring a steady supply of clean water. Electric utilities encompass power generation plants-using coal, natural gas, nuclear, and renewable sources-along with electrical grids, substations, and transformers to distribute electricity efficiently. Gas utilities feature natural gas extraction facilities, pipelines, storage facilities, and distribution networks, providing a key energy source for heating and industry. Telecommunication utilities support connectivity through infrastructure for landline and mobile phone networks, internet service providers, and cable networks, enabling communication and access to digital resources across the city.

Services

Services form the operational layer of urban infrastructure, delivering safety, financial stability, and human support. Public services include police stations, fire stations, emergency response services, and government offices providing administrative services, maintaining order and assisting citizens in times of need. Financial services are provided by banks, ATMs, credit unions, and financial institutions offering loans and other financial support, facilitating economic transactions and security. Healthcare services involve medical practitioners, specialists, therapists, and ancillary services like diagnostics and rehabilitation, ensuring comprehensive health care delivery. Education services consist of teachers, instructors, tutors, counselors, and support staff, driving the educational system and supporting student success through direct engagement and guidance.

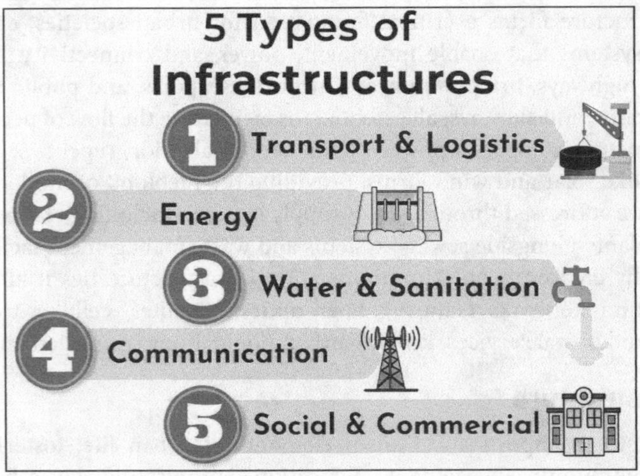

Figure 3.1: *Types of Infrastructure*

3.1.1 Significance and Importance

he importance of infrastructure extends beyond mere functionality, deeply influencing economic, social, and environmental outcomes in urban settings. Efficient transportation and energy systems boost productivity and attract investment, while access to education and healthcare elevates personal development and longevity, directly impacting quality of life. Safety is reinforced through well-designed roads and emergency services, protecting communities from harm, whereas sustainable infrastructure like renewable energy and green spaces combats climate change. Social cohesion thrives in community centers and parks, fostering civic engagement, and equitable access to these resources reduces disparities across socioeconomic groups, ensuring inclusivity. Additionally, modern infrastructure supports global competitiveness by enabling innovation through cutting-edge telecom and research facilities, underscoring its multifaceted role in building prosperous urban societies.

3.2 DATA REQUIREMENTS FOR URBAN PLANNING

Effective urban transportation planning hinges on a rich tapestry of data that informs decision-making and resource allocation. Planners rely on population data-size, growth rates, demographics, and density-to understand the scale and distribution of mobility needs. Land use data, including zoning and patterns, reveals how residential, commercial, and recreational spaces shape travel demand, while an inventory of existing infrastructure like roads, utilities, and telecom networks highlights current capacities. Transportation data, such as traffic volumes, vehicle ownership, and transit ridership, paints a picture of usage patterns, complemented by environmental data on air quality, noise, and hazard risks to assess sustainability challenges. Economic and social data, covering employment hubs, income levels, crime rates, and service access, contextualize broader urban dynamics, while technological data on broadband and smart city tools like IoT devices signal readiness for innovation. Policy frameworks and future growth projections further guide planners in anticipating long-term needs, ensuring that data-driven strategies optimize efficiency, enhance livability, and promote sustainable urban development.

3.2.1 Key Data Categories

The breadth of data required spans multiple domains, each critical to holistic planning. Population statistics detail who needs transport, while land use data maps where they travel, and infrastructure inventories show what systems support them. Transportation metrics reveal how people move, environmental data flags ecological impacts, and economic indicators pinpoint activity hubs driving demand. Social data uncovers accessibility gaps, and technological insights highlight tools for smart solutions, collectively enabling planners to craft informed, equitable, and forward-looking urban networks.

3.3 RESOURCE ANALYSIS FOR SMART TRANSPORTATION

Resource analysis in smart urban transportation systems is a strategic process to optimize efficiency, sustainability, and resilience. It begins with collecting real-time data from sensors and GPS to analyze traffic patterns and demand, leveraging analytics and machine learning for route and resource optimization. Existing infrastructure-roads, bridges, and transit systems-is assessed to pinpoint upgrade needs, integrating smart solutions like intelligent traffic signals and parking systems. Vehicle fleets are evaluated for performance, with tracking and predictive maintenance minimizing downtime, while energy analysis drives adoption of electric vehicles and renewables to cut emissions. Financial feasibility is weighed through cost-benefit studies, tapping into grants and partnerships, and human capital is bolstered with training for tech-driven systems. Regulatory frameworks are reviewed to encourage innovation, and community feedback ensures solutions align with local needs, creating a holistic approach that enhances urban mobility and environmental health.

3.3.1 Core Components of Analysis

Key components include data for real-time insights, infrastructure for physical upgrades, and vehicles for operational efficiency. Energy strategies focus on sustainability, financial planning secures funding, and human skills adapt to new tech. Regulations facilitate progress, and stakeholder collaboration ensures relevance, together building a robust transportation ecosystem.

3.4 INFRASTRUCTURE PROVISION IN SMART SYSTEMS

Providing infrastructure for smart urban transportation involves deploying cutting-edge technologies to boost mobility and sustainability. Digital foundations like high-speed internet and IoT sensors enable real-time traffic monitoring, while Intelligent Transportation Systems (ITS) optimize flow with dynamic signals and signage. Smart mobility hubs integrate transit modes, offering amenities like EV charging and real-time info, and public transit upgrades-contactless payments, priority lanes-enhance reliability. Active transportation infrastructure, such as bike lanes and sidewalks, promotes cycling and walking, supported by smart bike-sharing apps.

Electric vehicle charging networks, incentivized by rebates, reduce fossil fuel reliance, and open data platforms ensure interoperability across systems. Resilience is built with backup systems to handle disruptions, creating an efficient, accessible network that elevates urban quality of life.

3.4.1 Key Features of Provision

Digital infrastructure powers connectivity, ITS improves traffic management, and mobility hubs link transport modes. Public transit gains efficiency, active options encourage health, and EV support cuts emissions. Data sharing fosters innovation, and resilience ensures continuity, forming a sustainable transport foundation.

3.5 ROLE OF TRANSPORT IN URBAN ECOSYSTEMS

Transportation is the lifeblood of smart urban systems, driving mobility, safety, and sustainability. It enhances accessibility through multimodal networks-public transit, biking, walking-connecting people seamlessly to destinations. Advanced technologies like real-time traffic monitoring and congestion pricing reduce travel times and gridlock, while safety is bolstered by connected vehicles and predictive analytics that preempt hazards. Sustainability is prioritized with clean vehicles and shared mobility cutting emissions, and data analytics optimize routes and resources for efficiency.

User experience improves with real-time transit updates via apps and kiosks, empowering informed travel choices. Economically, reliable transport links jobs, schools, and amenities, boosting livability and competitiveness, making it a catalyst for thriving urban communities.

3.5.1 Contributions to Urban Life

Transport enhances mobility with diverse options, reduces congestion with smart tech, and ensures safety through innovation. It promotes sustainability, leverages data for efficiency, and improves user experience with timely info. It drives economic vitality and livability, shaping vibrant cities.

3.6 SMART TRANSPORTATION: DEFINITION AND MECHANISMS

Smart transportation represents a transformative approach to urban mobility, integrating advanced technologies to enhance efficiency, safety, and sustainability. It employs tools like car navigation, traffic signal control, speed cameras, and container management systems, drawing on real-time data from diverse sources to optimize travel. Experts at the 2019 New York Smart Cities event identified three pillars: infrastructure, sharing, and government support. Infrastructure leverages data-driven tools for fleet planning, while sharing-via ride-sharing and bike-sharing-boosts accessibility across social strata. Governments play a crucial role by enabling app-based, on-demand mobility through supportive policies and infrastructure investments.

Operationally, smart systems collect data via sensors and GPS, transmit it rapidly for analysis using AI, and relay updates to travelers through apps and signs. This synergy reduces congestion, improves safety by minimizing human error, and enhances quality of life, positioning smart transportation as a cornerstone of modern urban ecosystems.

3.6.1 Operational Framework

Smart transportation operates through data collection from hardware like cameras and sensors, tracking traffic in real time. Data is swiftly transmitted to management centers, analyzed with AI for insights, and shared with users via passenger information systems. This process cuts travel times, boosts safety with autonomous tech, and supports eco-friendly transit options, ensuring efficient urban mobility.

3.7 TYPES OF TRANSPORT SYSTEMS IN SMART CITIES

Smart urban transportation systems integrate a variety of transport modes, each optimized for efficiency and sustainability within cities. Public transit includes Bus Rapid Transit (BRT) with dedicated lanes, metro systems for high-capacity travel, Light Rail Transit (LRT) for frequent stops, trams for local routes, and commuter rail linking suburbs. Shared mobility offers ride-sharing platforms like Uber, car-sharing programs, bike-sharing for short trips, and scooter-sharing for last-mile connectivity. Active transportation promotes walking with enhanced sidewalks and cycling via protected bike lanes, fostering health and reducing emissions.

Emerging technologies like autonomous vehicles (AVs) promise safer roads, electric vehicles (EVs) cut fossil fuel use, and high-speed options like Hyperloop and Maglev revolutionize intercity travel. Intelligent Transportation Systems (ITS) tie these together with real-time traffic management, travel info services, and smart parking, creating a seamless, sustainable urban mobility network.

Figure 3.2: Types of Transport Systems in Smart Cities

3.7.1 Diverse Modal Integration

Public transit provides reliable mass movement, shared mobility offers flexible options, and active modes encourage sustainability. Emerging tech like AVs and EVs innovates travel, while ITS enhances coordination with traffic and parking solutions. This mix ensures accessibility, reduces congestion, and supports green urban living.

3.8 EVOLUTION OF TRANSPORTATION THROUGH HISTORY

The evolution of transportation reflects human ingenuity adapting to societal needs across millennia, shaping modern smart systems. Early humans relied on animals like horses and mules, transitioning to wheeled carts after the wheel's invention around 3500 BCE, easing long-distance travel. Waterways progressed from wooden logs to boats, then engine-powered ships, expanding trade. Roadways evolved from animal-drawn carriages to cycles and motor cars by the 17th century, with the internal combustion engine (1906) powering today's vehicles. Railways, starting 500 years ago with horse-pulled wooden rails, advanced to steam trains (1820), electric trains, and bullet trains by the 20th century. Airways began with hot air balloons, culminating in the Wright brothers' 1903 flight, leading to modern jets. Today's digital revolution introduces smart systems, autonomous vehicles, and renewable energy, driving sustainable urban transport forward.

3.8.1 Milestones in Transport Development

Animal transport gave way to wheeled vehicles, waterways scaled from logs to ships, and roadways modernized with engines. Railways shifted from wood to electric power, airways soared from balloons to jets, and digital tech now fuels smart, eco-conscious systems, marking a dynamic evolution.

3.9 TRANSPORT PROBLEMS AND MOBILITY CHALLENGES

Urban transportation faces multifaceted problems and mobility issues that challenge sustainability and equity. Traffic congestion, driven by population growth and inadequate road capacity, increases travel times and pollution, while vehicle emissions contribute to air quality degradation and health risks like respiratory diseases. Accessibility remains unequal, with low-income groups, the elderly, and disabled facing limited transit options, restricting access to jobs and services. Road safety is compromised by speeding and poor infrastructure, causing fatalities, and public transit often suffers from underfunding, leading to overcrowding and unreliability.

Last-mile connectivity lags in suburban areas, environmental impacts from greenhouse gases persist, urban sprawl fosters car dependency, and new tech like autonomous vehicles raises regulatory hurdles. Addressing these requires holistic solutions blending infrastructure, policy, and community collaboration.

3.9.1 Key Issues Impacting Mobility

Congestion and pollution strain urban systems, accessibility gaps hinder equity, and safety risks demand attention. Transit inefficiencies, last-mile gaps, environmental harm, sprawl, and tech disruptions complicate mobility, necessitating integrated strategies for resilient cities.

3.10 URBAN FORM AND TRANSPORT PATTERNS

Urban form profoundly influences transport patterns, dictating how residents move and interact within cities. High-density, mixed-use areas shorten travel distances, encouraging walking, cycling, and transit use, while low-density sprawl fosters car dependency and longer commutes.

Well-designed transport infrastructure-multimodal networks, bike lanes, and pedestrian paths-shapes sustainable mode choices, and Transit-Oriented Development (TOD) boosts transit ridership by clustering vibrant hubs near stations. Street designs with wide sidewalks and crosswalks enhance walkability, whereas car-centric layouts deter it.

Parking policies, like pricing or maximums, curb car use, and socioeconomic factors--income and housing-impact access to options. Emerging tech, such as ride-sharing and electric scooters, reshapes patterns, offering both opportunities and challenges for equitable, efficient urban mobility.

3.10.1 Factors Shaping Patterns

Density drives transit use, infrastructure guides mode choice, and TOD links land and transport. Street design affects walkability, parking influences car reliance, and socioeconomic disparities limit access. Tech innovations redefine mobility, blending efficiency with regulatory complexity.

3.11 THE LAND USE-TRANSPORT CYCLE

The land use-transport cycle illustrates the dynamic interplay between urban land use and transportation systems, shaping city development and mobility. It begins with land use planning, where zoning and development decisions designate areas for housing, commerce, and recreation, influencing where people live and work. These choices drive the development of transportation infrastructure-roads, transit lines, and bike paths-tailored to connect these zones efficiently.

Accessibility emerges as a key outcome, determining how easily residents reach jobs, schools, and services, which in turn affects their transportation mode choices, such as driving, walking, or taking transit. Travel behavior and demand shift based on this interplay, creating a feedback loop: new transit lines spur development along corridors, while concentrated employment zones increase transport needs. Over time, this cycle molds urban form, fostering compact, transit-friendly communities or sprawling, car-dependent suburbs, highlighting the need for integrated planning to enhance sustainability and livability.

3.11.1 Stages of the Cycle

Land use sets spatial patterns, infrastructure meets connectivity needs, and accessibility shapes travel options. Mode choices reflect infrastructure quality, driving behavior influences demand, and feedback loops adjust both systems. This process defines urban growth, balancing efficiency and sustainability.

3.12 HIERARCHY, CAPACITY, AND GEOMETRIC DESIGN OF ROADS

Roads and intersections are vital to urban transport, designed with hierarchy, capacity, and geometry to ensure safety and efficiency. The hierarchy classifies roads into highways for long-distance travel, arterials for high traffic, collectors linking neighborhoods, and local streets for property access, each with distinct speed and access rules. Capacity measures a road's ability to handle vehicle volumes, influenced by lane numbers, widths, and signal timing, assessed via Level of Service (LOS) from A (free flow) to F (severe congestion). Geometric design governs alignment-curves and grades for safe navigation-and cross-sections like lane widths and medians for vehicle separation.

Intersections feature turning radii and channelization to minimize conflicts, paired with traffic controls like signals and signs. This structured approach accommodates current and future needs, balancing functionality with safety and accessibility across urban landscapes.

3.12.1 Design Elements

Hierarchy defines road roles, capacity sets traffic limits, and alignment ensures safe paths. Cross-sections support diverse vehicles, intersections streamline flow, and controls regulate movement. Together, they optimize transport networks for urban demands.

3.13 URBAN TRANSPORT PLANNING PROCESS

Urban transport planning is a systematic effort to enhance mobility while addressing transport, environmental, and safety challenges. It starts with data collection-traffic patterns, emissions, and crash stats-to map existing conditions, followed by a needs assessment identifying congestion, pollution, and risk hotspots. Goals are set to reduce gridlock, cut emissions, and boost safety, guiding strategies like mode shift campaigns promoting transit and cycling, or demand management via congestion pricing.

Environmental measures include green infrastructure and low-emission zones, while safety interventions feature traffic calming and enforcement. Implementation turns plans into action-upgrading transit, building bike lanes-followed by monitoring to evaluate outcomes and adjust approaches. This process ensures cities evolve sustainably, balancing mobility with ecological and human well-being.

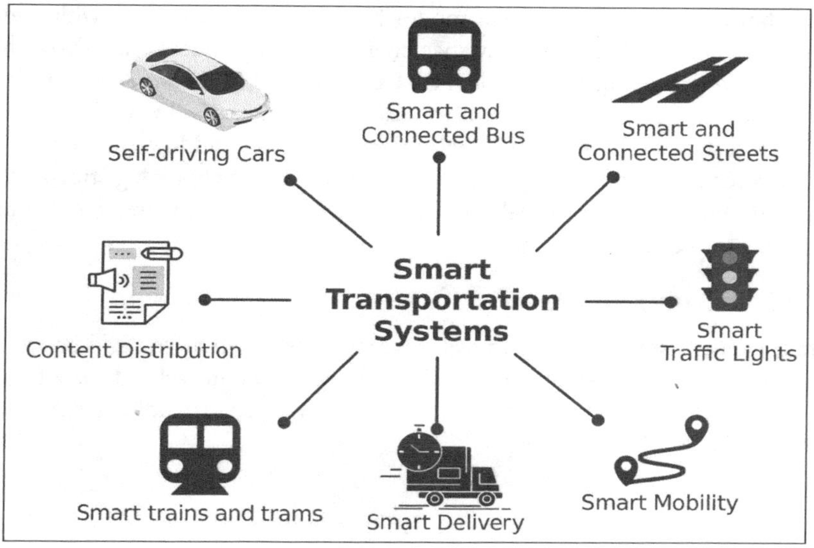

Figure 3.3: *Urban Transport Planning Process*

3.13.1 Key Phases

Data reveals current states, needs pinpoint issues, and goals set targets. Strategies shift behaviors, mitigation curbs impacts, and safety upgrades protect users. Implementation executes plans, and monitoring refines results, fostering livable urban spaces.

3.14 PRINCIPLES AND APPROACHES OF TRAFFIC MANAGEMENT

Traffic management orchestrates urban flow, blending principles and innovative approaches to enhance mobility and safety. It adopts an integrated, multimodal lens, designing systems for cars, pedestrians, cyclists, and transit to coexist seamlessly. Demand management-tolls, parking fees-curbs congestion, while traffic calming like speed humps slows vehicles in sensitive zones, prioritizing vulnerable users. Signal optimization, aided by adaptive controls, smooths traffic flow, and Intelligent Transportation Systems (ITS) deliver real-time monitoring via cameras and signs. Public transit gains priority with dedicated lanes, safety improves through intersection upgrades, and environmental goals promote electric vehicles and green designs. Community engagement ensures local buy-in, aligning strategies with resident needs, creating efficient, safe, and sustainable urban transport networks.

3.14.1 Core Strategies

Integration links modes, demand tools ease peak loads, and calming enhances safety. Signals and ITS boost efficiency, transit priority shifts reliance, and safety measures cut risks. Eco-focus reduces harm, and engagement tailors solutions, optimizing traffic.

3.15 TRANSPORT SYSTEM MANAGEMENT (TSM)

Transport System Management (TSM) leverages technology and strategy to streamline urban mobility, focusing on efficiency, safety, and sustainability. It optimizes traffic with signal timing and congestion pricing, enhances public transit via expanded networks and accessibility, and promotes active modes like walking and cycling with dedicated infrastructure. Transport Demand Management (TDM) reduces car trips through ridesharing and telecommuting, while ITS technologies-traffic cameras, traveler info systems-provide real-time control. Infrastructure is maximized with road upgrades and maintenance, sustainability is advanced with electric vehicles and low-emission tech, and safety is reinforced through calming and audits. Used by businesses for logistics or cities for planning, TSM cuts costs, speeds delivery, and boosts resilience, making it a vital tool for modern urban transport ecosystems.

3.15.1 TSM Components

Traffic management smooths flow, transit upgrades offer alternatives, and active modes cut emissions. TDM shifts demand, ITS enables precision, and infrastructure optimization leverages assets. Sustainability and safety focus ensure eco-friendly, secure systems, enhancing urban life.

◆◆◆

UNIT 4

Smarter City Management and Smarter Human Services

4.1 SMARTER OPERATIONS

Smarter operations are a revolutionary way of governing cities and providing human services, leveraging the potential of technology, data, and strategic innovation to build more efficient, sustainable, and responsive urban environments that serve citizens better. As cities become more complex—facing growing populations, aging infrastructure, and climate change—business as usual no longer suffices. Smarter operations respond to these issues by incorporating devices such as data analytics, the Internet of Things (IoT), and automation into the fabric of the city, allowing cities to predict issues, maximize resources, and improve quality of life. This section delves into the complex elements of smarter operations, demonstrating how they interact to create cities that prosper in today's world.

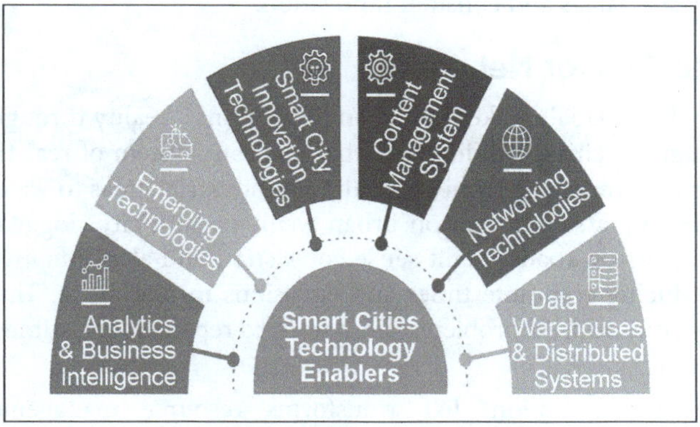

Figure 4.1: *Smarter Operations*

The key to smarter operations is that they can transition from reactive to proactive management. Instead of waiting for a blackout to repair the grid or a traffic jam to divert buses, cities can employ real-time data and predictive models to anticipate problems. This network-based system impacts all corners of urban life, from energy distribution to waste management, eliminating silos that previously hampered efficiency. For instance, a city could employ sensors to track water consumption and modulate supply in times of drought, while also cutting waste and spreading access. By combining technological advancement with strategic vision, smarter operations provide a platform for sustainable urban development that is to the benefit of both the present and the future.

4.1.1 Data Analytics and Predictive Insights

Data analysis is the foundation of wiser operations, converting the deluge of data cities produce into useful insights. Urban areas generate massive data sets every day—GPS app traffic speeds, smart meter energy use, even social media gossip about local issues. Analyzing this, managers can derive insights from patterns. Consider a busy downtown: analytics could show that pedestrian crashes peak at specific intersections during rush hour, leading to the installation of more intelligent crosswalks with adaptive signals. This data-driven method ensures resources are allocated where they're most needed, with maximum impact and minimum guesswork.

Predictive analytics takes it a step further by predicting future demand, enabling cities to plan ahead instead of just responding. Think of a public health agency monitoring flu tweets and pharmacy purchases to forecast an outbreak weeks ahead. Based on this knowledge, officials might stockpile vaccine, warn schools, and conduct awareness campaigns, containing the spread before it bursts hospital resources. Predictive models can also foresee infrastructure stress—e.g., a bridge that is about to reach capacity for holiday travel—initiating proactive repairs or rerouting traffic. This forward-thinking mentality not only enhances day-to-day operations but also enhances resilience to disruptions, ranging from natural catastrophes to economic changes, making cities more resilient in an uncertain world.

The elegance of these tools is their scalability. A small town may employ analytics to streamline its single bus route, while a city can plan an entire transportation network. Both scenarios yield the same outcome: improved services, reduced expenses, and more satisfied citizens. But it all depends on quality data and smart interpretation—garbage in, garbage out, goes the maxim. Cities need to spend money on reliable systems and educated staff to make sure insights are reliable and useful, a task that highlights the necessity of cooperation with technology specialists and constant innovation.

4.1.2 IoT and Sensor Networks

The Internet of Things (IoT) makes intelligent operations a reality through the embedding of sensors throughout cities, building an urban nervous system of real-time information. These sensors track everything from air quality in industrial areas to water levels in storm water drains, keeping a steady beat on urban wellness. In a city clogged with traffic, for example, IoT sensors on roads might sense congestion and alert adaptive traffic lights to smooth flow, reducing commute times and emissions in one move. This responsiveness changes the way cities address problems, from delayed repairs to real-time adjustments that keep systems running.

Outside of transportation, IoT transforms resource management. Imagine a neighbourhood where garbage cans beep when they are full, enabling waste trucks to bypass empty stops and conserve fuel—a small change with substantial savings in the long run. In another example, air sensors can alert during smog surges, closing schools to keep children indoors while officials crack down on polluters. Safety is also improved: sensors in old bridges can spot micro fractures, preventing collapses before they occur. These applications illustrate how IoT converts fixed infrastructures into dynamic assets, improving efficiency and saving lives.

Implementation, though, is not without challenges. Sensor network installation and upkeep require huge initial investment, and rural or budget-constrained regions risk falling behind. Privacy issues are also at stake—citizens may resist round-the-clock monitoring, concerned about data abuse. Cities need to weigh these trade-offs against clear policies and fair rollout plans that make IoT accessible to all communities. Implemented correctly, this technology spins a web of connectivity that renders urban operations more intelligent, secure, and sustainable.

4.1.3 Smart Infrastructure and Automation

Smart infrastructure is the physical foundation of smarter operations, embedding advanced technologies into the systems that energize cities. Smart grids are a prime example, matching electricity usage with supply in real time by drawing on renewable sources such as solar or wind. In the midst of a heatwave, a smart grid could redirect non-essential usage—such as pool pumps—to off-peak times, avoiding blackouts while keeping houses cool. Analogously, intelligent transportation systems take advantage of information to streamline bus routes or time traffic lights to minimize congestion and fuel consumption along sprawling metropolitan road networks.

Robots and computers enhance these advantages by automating mundane tasks to allow human employees to play important strategic roles. In waste recovery, robotic grapples in recycling facilities are able to segregate plastics and paper more rapidly than any individual, increasing yields and reducing the use of landfill space. On urban roads, self-governing drones could scan electrical lines or carry vital supplies, navigating around traffic to access distant zones in a short time. Such innovations do not only save time—they save costs and reduce errors, enabling cities to make more out of every budget. A sanitation department, for example, could transfer the savings from robotized waste collection to improving park facilities, bettering community amenities.

The ripple effects spread to sustainability. Intelligent buildings with smart lighting and HVAC systems cut energy consumption, while robot maintenance teams increase infrastructure life, postponing expensive replacements. But automation also raises concerns about employment—will it replace workers or produce new jobs in tech management? Cities need to couple these technologies with retraining initiatives to keep everyone included. When used judiciously, smart infrastructure and automation are an unstoppable pair, fuelling efficiency and resilience equally.

4.1.4 Citizen Resilience and Engagement

Smarter operations are not about technology alone—about people. Citizen engagement makes city systems more responsive, utilizing digital platforms to collect input and establish trust. A resident may report a water-logged street through an app, which may activate a prompt response while monitoring the progress online. Two-way communication gives power to communities, making them active participants in urban management. In a sea town, say, residents would decide on designs for flood barriers, so that solutions take their priorities and life experience into account.

Resilience planning makes this participation loop back to stability over the longer term, as cities are equipped for disasters such as storms or economic collapse. Historical flood records might inform emergency shelter placement, while drills among citizens make family members familiar with evacuation routes. In a pandemic, a city can use feedback to tailor mask distribution, starting with hardest-hit neighbourhoods. This forward-thinking approach reduces damage and accelerates recovery, as educated residents augment official efforts. Resilience also involves coping with chronic stressors—such as sea level rise—by investing in measures like raised roads or parks that serve as flood buffers.

Together, engagement and resilience form a self-reinforcing cycle. Open operations foster public trust, which in turn spurs cooperation in times of adversity. There are challenges, however: digital divides can leave behind low-income or older residents, and resilience plans need funding that financially strapped cities may not have. Closing these gaps with outreach and innovative financing—such as public-private partnerships—makes smarter operations truly accessible to all, combining human touch with technological savvy.

4.2 FACILITATING CROSS-AGENCY INTEGRATION

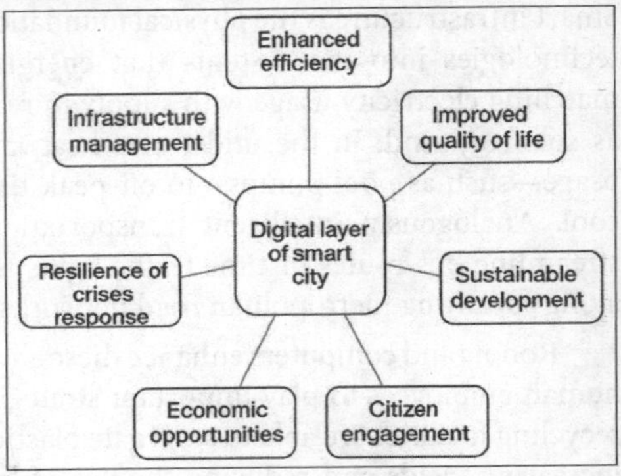

Figure 4.2: *Digital Layer of Smart City*

Cross-agency integration is what holds together smart city management and human services together, coordinating disjointed government agencies into a collaborative whole. Agency silos that previously existed among entities such as transportation, health, and safety replicated efforts or lost opportunities for cooperation. Integration tears down the barriers, generating coordination that deals with multifaceted urban challenges—such as housing emergencies or disaster relief—more efficiently than individual agencies alone could. This part explores approaches that enable this to happen, demonstrating how cities can integrate an unbroken tapestry of services that empower people.

The stakes are high: fragmented systems squander resources and create gaps in care, whereas integrated ones provide end-to-end solutions. A family at risk of eviction, for example, may require housing assistance, employment support, and medical care—needs that cut across agencies. By coordinating efforts, cities can tackle such challenges holistically, enhancing outcomes and efficiency. Technology, training, and partnerships power this change, building a system where collaboration is not an ideal but a pragmatic reality that reshapes urban life.

4.2.1 Shared Data Platforms and Integrated Models

Shared data platforms are the technical foundation of cross-agency integration, facilitating smooth information exchange across departments. Imagine a city where social workers use transit schedules to transport clients to job interviews, or police use health records to help someone in a mental health crisis. These platforms leverage common standards—such as standardized APIs—to provide compatibility, while encryption safeguards privacy. In practice, this could be a dashboard of currently available hospital beds in real time during a flu outbreak, communicated between health, emergency, and transport departments to align care and routes for ambulances.

Integrated service delivery models take it a step further by combining agency resources into single solutions. In a city fighting youth violence, schools, police, and counselors could collaborate through one case management system, providing tutoring, patrolling, and therapy as a bundle. This strategy slashes red tape—families don't have to work through different bureaucracies—and increases impact by treating root causes in a comprehensive way. A pilot in a single city reduced dropout rates by 20% after bringing together education and social services, demonstrating the potential of synergy. To scale this, it takes investment in technology and building trust among agencies, but the reward is a city that functions as one.

4.2.2 Collaboration and Training

Cooperation succeeds when agency workers see each other's worlds, so cross-training is a key to integration. A workshop with transit planners and healthcare providers may uncover the effect of bus tardiness on clinic no-shows, triggering cooperative solutions such as shuttle buses. This mutual information dissolves turf battles, substituting cooperation for competition. When training emergency personnel with utility crews in a flood area, restoring power after the storm can become more efficient as each learns about the other's limitations and resources.

Joint planning solidifies this unity, uniting agencies to establish common objectives. Routine strategy meetings—perhaps to reduce carbon emissions—may have transport officials promote electric buses while energy teams increase charging points, coordinating efforts for optimal impact. In one city, a task force involving multiple agencies reduced homelessness by half by combining housing, health, and employment resources, something no single department could do. These tasks take time and leadership but render agencies into one integrated body with enhanced individual and combined outreach and responsiveness.

4.2.3 Technology and Community Engagement

Technology powers integration through supplying mechanisms for synchronization of efforts within agencies. One shared virtual space could enable teachers and child welfare workers to monitor a pupil's attendance and record truancy for timely intervention. In a wildfire, a single app could manage firefighters, medics, and road crews, conducting evacuations and relief with seamless flow. Such systems eliminate lag and mistakes, making teamwork instinctive. One city employing this technology reduced response times by 15% during crises, demonstrating its effectiveness.

Community engagement infuses a personal touch, such that integration accommodates actual requirements. Public meetings in which citizens bring to the fore problems—such as potholes or crime—inform agency priorities, while Internet surveys may influence the design of a new transit centre. In a low-income neighbourhood, an alliance of citizens, health workers, and community groups could collaboratively develop a mobile clinic, combining neighbourhood understanding with agency heft. Such engagement engenders trust and accountability, though it demands efforts at outreach to represent marginalized communities. In tandem, technology and community connections create an integration model that's cutting-edge yet rooted in experience.

4.3 SMARTER WATER MANAGEMENT

Water supports cities, so smarter water management is a critical gear in urban and human service systems. With climate change fueling droughts and floods, and urbanization stretching supplies, cities need to reimagine how they manage this precious resource. More intelligent water management applies technology, data, and sustainable solutions to provide clean, dependable water while reducing waste and expenses. This chapter looks at how cities can develop strong water systems that promote health, economies, and environments, resilient to today's challenges and uncertainties of the future.

The problem is overwhelming: leaks shed billions of gallons annually, pollution endangers ecosystems, and demand tends to exceed supply. Smarter strategies push back with real-time tracking, predictive analytics, and community engagement, transforming water systems into proactive networks. From sensors detecting pipe bursts to rain gardens reducing runoff, these solutions demonstrate how innovation can protect a resource that touches every aspect of urban life.

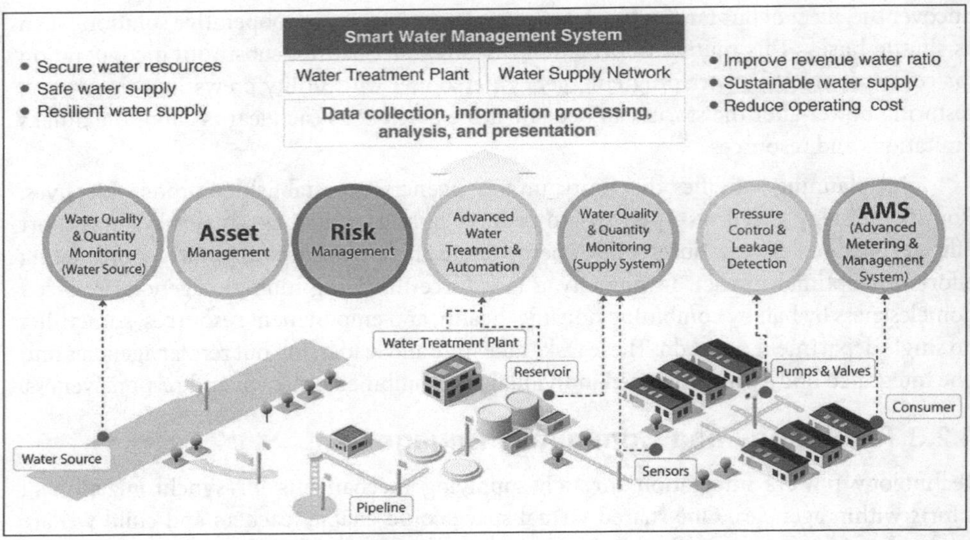

Figure 4.3: Smart Water Management System

4.3.1 Technology and Infrastructure Upgrades

Technology grounds wiser water management, with devices such as digital meters and sensors offering a glimpse into usage and system condition. In a sprawling suburb, smart meters could alert a homeowner's leaky faucet, leading to a repair that saves thousands of gallons. Acoustic sensors, on the other hand, identify underground pipe breaks, reducing repair delays— one city reduced water loss 25% this way. These machines input into SCADA systems, which remotely adjust pumps and valves to meet demand, providing constant flow without overloading infrastructure.

Smart infrastructure upgrades this further. Sewers fitted with sensors forecast wear, while treatment plants respond to rain forecasts, preventing overflows. Green infrastructure—such as permeable pavements or wetlands—captures rainwater, lowering flood risk and recharging aquifers. In a rainy town, such interventions may make the streets dry while watering parks naturally. These improvements require investment, but the long-term dividends—fewer emergencies, lower costs—make them a smart bet for water security and sustainability.

4.3.2 Conservation and Community Participation

Conservation balances tech with behavior to stretch water resources. Cities may provide rebates for low-flow showerheads or apps presenting day-to-day use, encouraging residents to reduce. In a drought, one city utilized meter data to send heavy users advice—such as night watering—reducing consumption 30%. These actions relax pressure on systems and empower households, demonstrating small tweaks make a difference. Education campaigns boost this, educating children about aquifers or homeowners about rain barrels, inculcating conservation in city life.

Community involvement makes the impact more profound. Greywater reuse workshops or water-saving idea contests—such as a school xeriscaping project—galvanize grassroots activity. In a desert metropolis, citizens may organize to construct a community cistern, combining resources with municipal funding. This engagement guarantees tech fixes endure, albeit outreach must cross language or income barriers to reach everyone. Through combining innovation with shared will, smarter water management forges a robust, water-conscious urban future.

4.4 SMARTER PUBLIC SAFETY

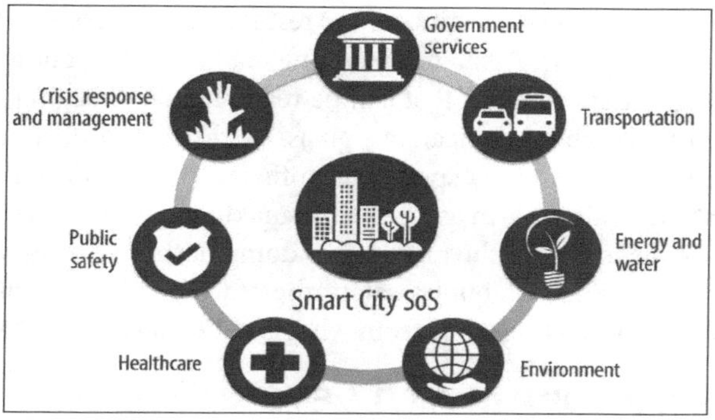

Figure 4.4: *Smarter Public Safety*

Public safety is the foundation of city vibrancy, influencing how safe and connected people are. Smarter public safety leverages technology, data, and social bonds to deter crime, accelerate emergency responses, and address root causes such as poverty or addiction. With cities experiencing increasing complexity—urban sprawl to climate catastrophes—they require technology-enabled overhauls of the traditional safety net. This section explains how smarter solutions safeguard citizens, combining proactive technologies with human-oriented strategies to create trust and resilience.

Safety's reach is broad, from street crime to mass crises, each requiring specific solutions. Smarter systems address this range with real-time information and coordinated efforts, so aid reaches quickly and prevention precedes reaction. By connecting police with social services and residents, cities weave a safety net that's high-tech and grounded in community requirements.

4.4.1 Data-Driven and Community-Based Strategies

Data-driven policing uses analytics to identify and deter crime. Plotting previous break-ins may show a cluster around a poorly lit park, leading to increased lighting and patrols— a city that did this saw theft fall 40%. Live surveillance, such as AI-screened CCTV, sees trouble in real time—say, a fight about to break out outside a bar—informing officers before it gets out of hand. These technologies make lean budgets go further, concentrating efforts where data indicates they'll be most valuable, though with the need for sensitive use to prevent profiling mistakes.

Community policing counterbalances this with people-to-people contact. Officers on foot beats or at safety fairs establish rapport, finding concerns—such as drug sales on a playground—stats may not. In a suburb, a citizen-police agreement to watch over abandoned lots reduced vandalism dramatically, as cooperation was spurred by trust. Merging social services—such as teen counselors—also suppresses crime by tackling its causes, reducing jail populations and mending communities. This combination of information and conversation builds a safety model that's accurate but intimate.

4.4.2 Emergency Response and Resilience

Intelligent emergency response uses technology to save lives and minutes. GPS-enabled fire engines could navigate around traffic to arrive at a fire, while a common dispatch system coordinates medics and police in a shooting. In an earthquake city, sensors detecting tremors could send immediate alerts, providing seconds to duck and cover. A city with one such area reduced response times 20% using these kinds of tools, their mettle in chaos. Agency-to-agency coordination—imagine power restored by utilities as victims are treated by medics—guarantees no delay. Resilience planning readies cities for larger dangers. Maps of risks could highlight areas to flood that can be ready for sandbagging, with evacuation exercises conducted with schools rehearsing plans. With a hurricane, an app delivering shelter notices keeps residents up to speed with officials. Preparation at the community level—such as first-aid training—magnifies this, making citizens part of the solution. Paying for it can be expensive, but the price tag of doing nothing—dead bodies, destroyed houses—is much higher. Smarter public safety therefore combines swift response with profound preparedness, protecting cities from what is anticipated and what is unexpected.

4.5 SMARTER BUILDINGS AND BEYOND

Smarter buildings transform city spaces, infusing efficiency, comfort, and resilience into the environments where people live, work, and play. As cities pursue energy targets and prepare for climate change, these buildings employ automation, renewables, and data to reduce waste and increase livability. This section discusses how smarter buildings make city management and human services better, with their impact extending to transform larger urban systems.

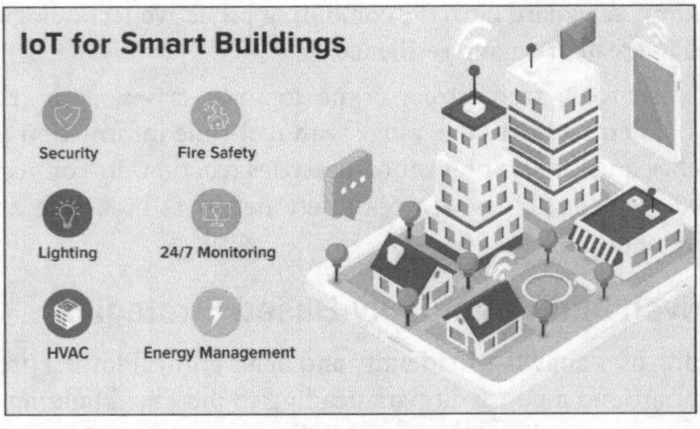

Figure 4.5: *IoT for Smart Buildings*

4.5.1 Energy Efficiency and Automation

Energy management systems (EMS) slim down buildings, with sensors to optimize power consumption. An office can dim the lights in vacant corridors or cool only active floors, based on real-time occupancy information— one tower reduced bills by 15% this way. Building automation systems (BAS) connect HVAC, lighting, and security into a single brain, allowing managers to adjust settings from afar. A school can secure unused wings at night while ventilating classrooms, keeping safety and savings in equilibrium easily. Renewables such as solar panels drive these gains, reducing fossil fuel dependence. A library that produces its own power may sell excess to the grid, smoothing peak loads. Predictive maintenance, through IoT sensors, identifies failing equipment—such as a wheezing AC—before it fails, extending equipment life. These capabilities reduce carbon footprints and expenses, although retrofitting existing buildings can be costly. Combined with incentives, smarter buildings become drivers of urban sustainability.

4.5.2 Benefits to Occupants and the Community

Activating occupants makes buildings collective undertakings. Apps displaying energy consumption may game out savings—tenants competing to reduce watts—while a green roof on a dorm acts as a student lab. Such participation enhances comfort and reduces waste, aligning individual behaviors with city objectives. In a heat wave, citizens adjusting thermostats based on app instructions can relieve grid pressure, a small gesture with significant effect. Outside walls, more intelligent buildings connect to urban networks. Integrated with smart grids, they modulate demand—reducing lighting during outages—balancing power across the city. During crises, a disaster-resistant clinic with solar power may provide care when lines go down. By interlacing efficiency with public service, these buildings improve human health, demonstrating buildings can be more than houses—they're critical pieces in wiser cities.

4.6 SMARTER HUMAN SERVICES

Smarter human services are at the core of a city's dedication to its citizens, using cutting-edge technologies and data-driven approaches to provide high-quality, accessible, and efficient assistance in education, healthcare, and social welfare. As cities become more diverse and needs change, conventional models of service—tied up in red tape and with limited reach—fail to keep up. Smarter human services bridge this gap by integrating tools such as IoT, digital platforms, and analytics into the fabric of service delivery, ensuring that cities not only meet basic needs but also empower individuals to thrive. This section explores

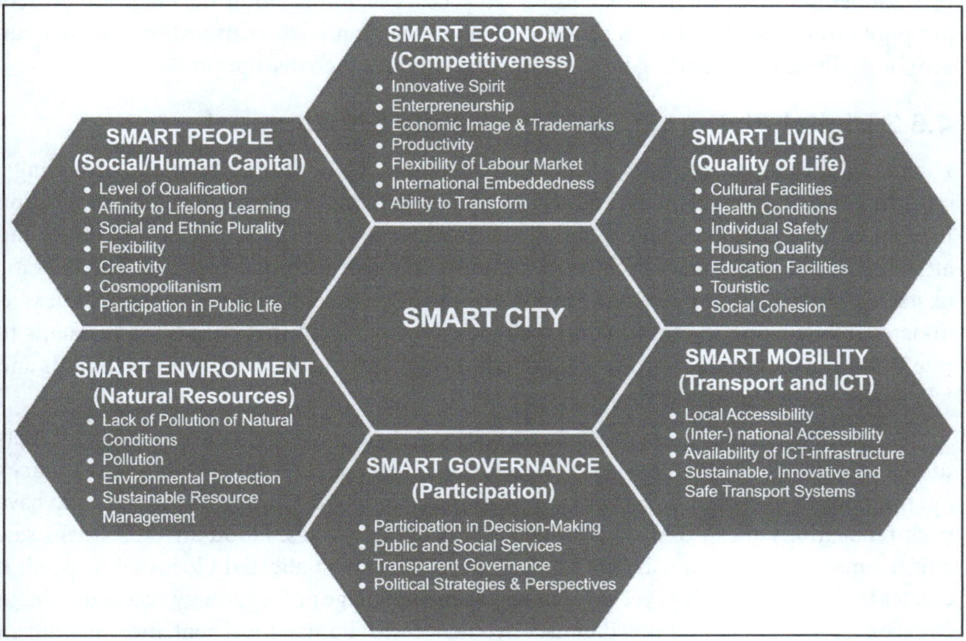

Figure 4.6: *Smarter Human Services*

how these innovations transform the way cities care for their people, creating systems that are responsive, equitable, and forward-thinking. The potential of smarter human services lies in their capacity to customize and streamline assistance. Instead of one-size-fits-all solutions, cities can make interventions—whether a telemedicine consultation for a homebound elderly person or job training for a jobless youth—tailored to real-time data and community feedback. This shift demands collaboration across sectors, robust privacy protections, and a focus on resilience to ensure services withstand crises like pandemics or economic downturns. From transportation to healthcare, the strategies outlined here illustrate how smarter human services elevate urban life, making cities not just places to live, but places to flourish.

4.6.1 Data Analytics and IoT Integration

Data analytics drives smarter human services by turning raw information into insights that shape policy and practice. Cities collect troves of data daily—school attendance records, hospital admissions, even utility usage—that reveal where services are succeeding or falling short. For instance, analyzing transit ridership might show that low-income families lack access to after-school programs, prompting targeted bus route expansions. Such specificity allocates resources to where they're needed the most, minimizing waste and increasing effect. For a mid-city population, it cut food bank wait times in half by identifying times of high demand, a modest adjustment for tremendous relief among low-income citizens.

The Internet of Things (IoT) scales this further by integrating live monitoring into systems of service. Air quality sensors outside schools might send asthma warnings to nurses, while intelligent traffic lights simplify ambulance paths to hospitals. In a high-density urban center, IoT streetlights may dim to conserve energy but illuminate when people walk by, finding a balance between safety and sustainability. These devices form a feedback loop—information comes in, changes go out—making services dynamic instead of static. Hindrances such as expensive setup costs or information overload are present but pilot projects such as a park sensor reducing irrigation waste demonstrate that IoT can economically scale, extending human services without much disruption.

4.6.2 Digital Platforms and Community Engagement

Digital platforms change the way that residents interact with human services, providing a one-stop shop for bill payments and service requests among other things. A city application may allow a parent to arrange a child's vaccination, request the repair of a pothole, and attend a virtual town hall—both from a phone. It is this ease that bypasses bureaucratic obstacles, particularly for active or mobility-impaired citizens, and increases openness as updates follow along in real time. In a single city, a platform that connected residents to free Wi-Fi hotspots reduced the digital divide, bringing thousands online to job boards and telehealth—a lifeline for the underserved.

Community involvement makes these platforms two-way streets, encouraging residents to help design the services they use. Web forums may collect feedback on a new library's opening hours, that they accommodate working parents' routines, while a poll may have park renovations ahead of road fixes depending on area votes. Flood-stricken towns saw citizens map damage using an app, delivering relief to most affected blocks with speed. It creates trust and ownership, yet cities need to close language or technology access divides to engage everyone. By combining digital convenience with human judgment, more intelligent human services become a collective endeavor, grounded in the community they serve.

4.6.3 Resilience and Cross-Sector Collaboration

Resilience planning makes human services weather-proof, from hurricanes to economic downturns. Predictive analytics may identify neighborhoods at risk of power loss, triggering pre-stocked food banks or mobile health clinics prior to a hurricane strike. During a pandemic, a city might leverage mobility data to redirect buses for vaccine distribution, ensuring shots continued to flow in the face of lockdowns. A coastal city reduced recovery time by 30% after a flood by pre-training volunteers and mapping vulnerable seniors—testament that preparation is worth it. Resilience is not simply about surviving; it's about preserving dignity and care when citizens need it most.

Cross-sector collaboration drives this by bringing together government, nonprofits, business, and schools to work on large problems. A unemployment surge could have job agencies, tech companies, and colleges initiate a coding bootcamp, sharing money and skills to retrain scores quickly. Elsewhere, a food access initiative connected grocers with pantries and transit to bring excess produce, cutting hunger rates in half. These collaborations multiply effect but demand defined roles and trust—turf wars can undermine even the best strategies. When working together, they create a safety net that's wide, rich, and agile, with smarter human services raising whole communities up.

4.7 SMARTER EDUCATION

Smarter education reinvents learning in cities, leveraging technology and data to make it more accessible, personalized, and effective—a critical component of human services. With city schools experiencing overcrowding, budget shortfalls, and varying student needs, mere traditional classrooms cannot keep pace.

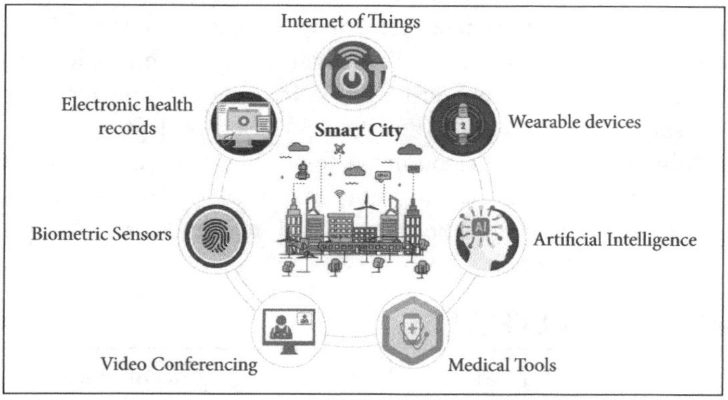

Figure 4.7: *Smart City*

Smarter education combines digital tools, data analytics, and local community feedback to close these gaps, getting students ready for an increasingly changing world while assisting educators and families. While briefly listed in the initial document under Smarter Human Services, its significance merits a more detailed discussion here, illustrating how it prepares cities to develop their future leaders. Urban success is dependent on the role of education: it fuels economic mobility, civic participation, and social unity. Smarter strategies build upon this by adjusting learning to each student's strengths—imagine a struggling reader that receives app-based practice while a math genius works out challenging problems online. This adaptability requires investment in technology and training but pays dividends in a generation prepared to innovate and respond, making the city more resilient as a whole.

4.7.1 Digital Learning and Analytics

Digital learning technology revolutionizes education by taking resources to students anywhere, anytime. Web-based platforms may provide video lessons for a child too sick to attend class, or virtual labs for schools with no science equipment. In a rural-belt city, a tablet initiative allowed children to learn coding despite having few teachers, leading to a 50% increase in STEM interest. These technologies even the playing field, although patchy internet or device availability can isolate some—cities need to subsidize technology to bridge this gap. Combined with face-to-face instruction, online learning produces a hybrid model that's scalable yet intimate. Analytics refines this further by monitoring progress and identifying needs. Metrics on test scores or attendance may indicate a third-grade reading dip, triggering additional tutors or parent workshops. In one school district, analytics identified chronic absenteeism linked to bus delays, prompting re-routed buses that increased attendance by 15%. Teachers are also winners—dashboards can identify which lessons resonate, honing their skills. Privacy threats are present, but anonymized data and transparent consent maintain trust. All together, these tools turn education into a precision endeavor, responding to each student's path.

4.7.2 Community and Resilience in Education

Community connections strengthen smarter education by connecting schools and neighborhood life. Parents may participate in online forums to select after-school activities, and companies sponsor teenagers learning trades such as plumbing or computer science. In an industrial town, an agreement with manufacturers supported robot clubs, getting graduates hired directly from high school. This connection makes sure the learning is relevant to work needs, although outreach has to extend to non-English speakers or working-class families to not exclude them. Schools become centers, not islands, of skill and belonging. Resilience secures schooling when disruption hits. Cloud backups ensure classes don't miss a beat in the blizzard, trauma training prepares instructors to counsel students after, say, a local shooting. The city stocked up on laptops ahead of an outage, so a student didn't miss a single lesson in the flood. Planning requires vision and money, yet it safeguards the right to learning, not luxury. More rational schooling therefore stitches together technology, neighborhood, and resilience, schooling students—and municipalities—on call for anything.

4.8 SMARTER HEALTHCARE

Smarter healthcare remakes urban wellness, leveraging technology and information to increase access, enhance outcomes, and reduce costs in human services. As cities grapple with aging populations, chronic illness, and healthcare inequality, conventional systems buckle under the pressure. Smarter healthcare responds with solutions such as telemedicine, predictive analytics, and wearables, providing care that is timely, customized, and cost-effective. This section explores how these technologies remake health services so that cities serve body and mind in a constantly changing environment. Healthcare's urban stakes are high: a sick population weighs down economies and spirits as well. Smarter strategies reduce this burden by reaching the underserved—consider a rural mom seeing a doctor over Zoom—or detecting illness early with data-driven alerts. Success depends on integration with other services and trust in tech, balancing innovation with empathy to heal communities whole.

4.8.1 Telemedicine and Predictive Analytics

Telemedicine shatters obstacles, delivering doctors to patients through screens. A diabetic in a bus-poor suburb may control blood sugar levels with an online nurse, avoiding a long commute. In an epidemic of the flu, a city's telemedicine clinic reduced ER visits 20%, freeing up crowded hallways. Far-off monitoring—e.g., heart sensors in the elderly—adds richness, warning medics of emergencies immediately. Expensive bandwidth and computer literacy hurdles present obstacles to roll-out, yet subsidies and instruction can expand outreach, putting care at a click. Predictive analytics predicts trouble before it happens. Computers processing hospital information may identify an at-risk teen who is liable to asthma attacks, and thus refill inhalers and send home visits. In a city choked with smog, this cut admissions in half, saving lives and money. Wearables such as fitness trackers input into this system, monitoring pulses or sleep to encourage healthier behavior—a runner may modify diet after a smartwatch alert. Fears of privacy still exist, but locked-down systems protect data. All together, these technologies transform healthcare from reaction to prevention, a breakthrough for urban health.

4.8.2 Patient Empowerment and Optimization of Resources

Patient empowerment sets patients in charge. Smartphones may allow a cancer patient to schedule chemo or text with a nurse, eliminating worry and forgotten doses. Health education—videos on nutrition or smoking danger—triggers action; a campaign reduced diabetes rates 10% after diet classes. Portals connecting patients to records guarantee they are their own care providers, though digital divides must be overcome with hotspots or free clinics. This agency increases adherence and trust, the building blocks of sustainable health benefits. Resource optimization means that healthcare goes further. Analytics may reveal a clinic's busiest times, bringing on staff then and cutting elsewhere—efficiency without burnout. In a stretched city, this balanced the load, treating 30% more patients annually. Health information exchanges synchronize records between hospitals, avoiding repeat tests—a heart patient's scan comes with them, accelerating treatment. These adjustments require initial tech but pay back with leaner, sharper care, powering healthier urban lives.

4.9 SMARTER SOCIAL SERVICES

More intelligent social services combine technology and empathy to serve the needy, a vital branch of human services in smarter cities. City problems such as homelessness, substance abuse, and poverty confound easy solutions, overburdening antiquated models of assistance. More intelligent social services respond with consolidated systems, analytics tools, and tele-access, providing assistance that is quick, targeted, and equitable. This chapter discusses how these approaches enrich lives, weaving a safety net that is both high-tech and humane.

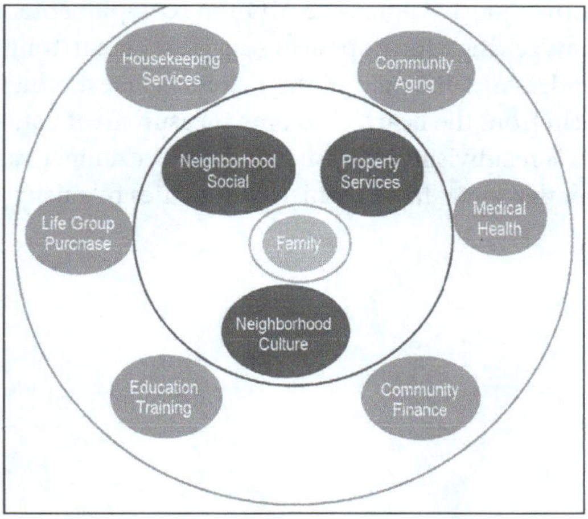

Figure 4.8: *Smarter Social Services*

Social services are the conscience of a city, an expression of its concern for the excluded. Smarter strategies amplify this by identifying threats early—such as a family on the brink of eviction—or linking clients to resources with a click. Cooperation and compassion ground these efforts, making sure tech complements, rather than supplants, the human touch that characterizes successful support.

4.9.1 Integrated Systems and Predictive Tools

Integrated case management systems consolidate aid, tying agencies together into one hub. A single mother could apply for housing, food stamps, and child care through a single portal, with social workers monitoring all needs in real time. In a test city, this reduced wait times by 40%, alleviating desperation. These systems share information securely—e.g., a doctor recording a client's depression—so that care is holistic without duplicative forms. Setup costs and staff training pose hurdles, but the payoff is a system that feels seamless to those it serves.

Predictive models identify crises before they break out. Analytics could alert a threatened vet to homelessness through rent increases and job loss, initiating rent assistance quickly. A single city's system identified 60% of vulnerable cases early, reducing shelter stays. Resource mapping increases reach—digital guides connect clients to soup kitchens or counsellors within reach, eliminating legwork. These proactive measures save dollars and suffering, albeit with careful data and follow-through to prevent false alarms or missed opportunities.

4.9.2 Remote Access and Community Support

Remote service provision brings assistance beyond the walls of offices. Virtual therapy may extend to a teen in a remote corner, while job fairs online bring the jobless into contact with opportunities—a lockdown scheme deployed 500 workers thus. Telehealth for addiction treatment keeps people on the recovery path, albeit patchy internet or device access restricts access to some. Subsidies and mobile units can fill such gaps, and assistance as ubiquitous as their clients.

Social backing and feedback keep services connected with actual needs. Online surveys can query clients regarding whether food aid satisfies dietary desires, adjusting the menu in turn—boosted uptake 25%. Online computer literacy drives equip the poor to join the digital fray, getting a job or benefit sooner. Webinar-trained staff, providing trauma-informed care, understand the pain of their clients—like a refugee with PTSD—enabling them to provide help from the heart. Outcome measurement confirms it works, demonstrating to funders a 15% recidivism decrease here or fewer hunger cases there. Combined, these create a wiser, gentler social fabric, which raises cities by raising their most vulnerable.

◆◆◆

UNIT 5

Smarter City and IoT

5.1 IoT FUNDAMENTALS

5.1.1 IoT Impact

The Internet of Things (IoT) has emerged as a cornerstone of the Fourth Industrial Revolution, radically changing the way individuals, organizations, and governments interact with technology and the environment. At its core, IoT refers to a network of physical objects—commonly known as "smart devices"—embedded with sensors, software, and communication capabilities that enable them to collect and exchange data. Unlike traditional computer-based networks, IoT extends connectivity to a wide range of everyday objects, from household appliances to industrial machinery, urban infrastructure, and healthcare devices.

The impact of IoT can be understood across four main dimensions: economic, social, technological and environmental.

In **Economic Impact**, IoT drives efficiency and cost reduction in almost every sector. By enabling predictive maintenance, industries can prevent equipment breakdowns and avoid costly downtime. In logistics and supply chain management, IoT devices track goods in real time, optimize delivery routes, and reduce waste. Smart farming uses IoT sensors to monitor soil moisture, weather conditions, and crop health, resulting in better yields and reduced input costs. Reports from market analysts predict that IoT could contribute trillions of dollars to the global economy by improving resource utilization and productivity.

In **Social Impact**. From the perspective of citizens, IoT enhances quality of life. Smart home devices such as connected thermostats, lighting systems, and appliances provide convenience and energy savings. Wearable health devices monitor vital signs, alert patients to potential health risks, and transmit data to doctors for better healthcare management. In urban areas, IoT applications such as intelligent traffic systems reduce congestion and air pollution, while smart waste bins improve cleanliness and efficiency of waste collection. Collectively, these applications contribute to healthier, safer, and more livable communities.

In **Technological Impact**, IoT also acts as a catalyst for innovation and technological advancement. It integrates seamlessly with other emerging technologies such as artificial intelligence (AI), machine learning (ML), blockchain, and edge computing. AI-powered IoT systems can analyze large volumes of data in real time, enabling smarter decision-making in critical sectors like transportation, manufacturing, and energy. For example, self-driving cars rely on IoT sensors combined with AI algorithms to navigate safely. Similarly, in energy grids, IoT devices combined with predictive analytics allow for demand forecasting and efficient power distribution.

In **Environmental Impact**, Another significant area of IoT's influence is sustainability. By enabling efficient use of resources, IoT helps reduce the environmental footprint of human activity. Smart grids balance electricity supply and demand, reducing energy waste. Connected water management systems monitor usage and detect leaks, conserving water. Smart street lighting systems adjust brightness according to real-time needs, significantly lowering electricity consumption. These initiatives not only save costs but also contribute toward achieving global sustainability goals such as reduced carbon emissions and better climate resilience.

5.2 IoT CONNECTIVITY

Connectivity forms the **nervous system of IoT**, enabling billions of devices to exchange data, coordinate actions, and provide real-time insights. Without reliable communication channels, IoT systems cannot function, regardless of how advanced their sensors or applications may be.

Connectivity in IoT can be broadly categorized into **wired** and **wireless technologies.** The choice of connectivity depends on factors such as deployment size, data requirements, cost constraints, and energy consumption.

5.2.1 Wired Connectivity

Ethernet is the most widely used wired technology in IoT. It offers high reliability, speed, and low latency, making it suitable for industrial IoT applications where large volumes of data must be transmitted securely. **Modbus** and **CAN Bus** are also used in specific industrial automation systems. However, wired solutions are **less flexible and more expensive** when scaling across large geographic areas, such as cities. This makes them less favorable for smart city deployments.

5.2.2 Wireless Connectivity

Wireless communication is the backbone of most IoT applications due to its **flexibility, scalability, and lower infrastructure cost.** Different wireless technologies cater to different requirements:

- **Wi-Fi**: Offers high bandwidth and is widely used in homes, offices, and hotspots. However, it has limited range and relatively high power consumption.
- **Zigbee**: A low-power, short-range technology used in home automation, industrial monitoring, and sensor networks. Zigbee supports mesh networking, enabling devices to relay data across a network.
- **LoRaWAN**: Designed for long-range, low-power communication. It is well-suited for city-wide applications such as smart street lighting and environmental monitoring.
- **NB-IoT (Narrowband IoT)**: Operates on licensed cellular spectrum, offering secure, low-power, and wide-area connectivity. Ideal for applications like utility metering and smart parking.
- **5G**: Provides ultra-low latency, massive device connectivity, and high bandwidth, enabling advanced applications such as autonomous vehicles and remote healthcare.

5.2.3 Hybrid Connectivity

In practical deployments, especially in smart cities, a **hybrid approach** is often adopted. For example :

- Smart homes may use **Zigbee** for internal device communication and **Wi-Fi** for internet backhaul.
- Smart traffic control systems may use **LoRaWAN** for low-power sensor communication but rely on **5G** for real-time video analytics.

Thus, connectivity is not about selecting one technology but creating an ecosystem where **different technologies complement one another** to achieve efficiency, scalability, and reliability.

5.3 IoT NETWORK ARCHITECTURE AND DESIGN

The architecture of an IoT network defines how devices, gateways, and applications interact to deliver services. A well-designed architecture ensures **seamless communication, efficient data processing, and secure service delivery**.

5.3.1 Three-Layer Architecture

The simplest model of IoT architecture consists of **three layers** :

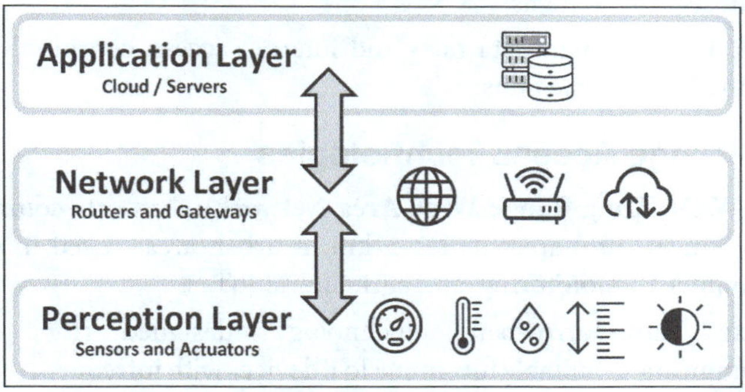

1. **Perception Layer**: Also known as the sensing layer, it includes sensors, actuators, RFID tags, and cameras. These devices collect data about the physical world.
2. **Network Layer**: Responsible for transmitting data from sensors to processing units using technologies like Wi-Fi, Bluetooth, Zigbee, LoRaWAN, or cellular networks.
3. **Application Layer**: Provides services to end-users, such as smart home applications, health monitoring dashboards, or traffic control systems.

This architecture is lightweight and suitable for small-scale IoT deployments.

5.3.2 Five-Layer Architecture

For large-scale smart city systems, a more **comprehensive five-layer architecture** is preferred:

1. **Perception Layer:** Sensing devices that capture data.
2. **Network Layer:** Communication protocols and technologies.
3. **Edge Layer:** Gateways and edge devices that filter and preprocess data before sending it to the cloud.

4. **Processing Layer** – Cloud platforms, big data analytics, and machine learning algorithms for decision-making.
5. **Application Layer** – User-facing applications that provide actionable insights.

This model is **scalable, flexible, and robust**, allowing efficient handling of vast amounts of city-wide data.

5.4 IoT ACCESS TECHNOLOGIES

Access technologies in IoT define how devices connect to networks. The choice of technology depends on **coverage area, power consumption, cost, and bandwidth requirements.** They are classified into **short-range** and **long-range** categories.

5.4.1 Short-Range Access Technologies

- **Bluetooth & BLE (Bluetooth Low Energy)**: Common in wearable devices and short-range personal IoT applications. BLE is energy-efficient, making it suitable for fitness trackers and medical sensors.
- **Zigbee**: Supports mesh networking and is widely used in home automation systems (smart lights, thermostats).
- **Z-Wave**: Similar to Zigbee but optimized for home control applications, often used in security systems.
- **Wi-Fi**: Provides high data rates and internet access, commonly used for smart appliances and home hubs.

5.4.2 Long-Range Access Technologies

- **LoRaWAN (Long Range Wide Area Network)**: Supports communication over 10–15 km in rural areas and 2–5 km in urban areas. Used in smart metering, environmental monitoring, and agricultural IoT.
- **Sigfox**: Ultra-narrowband technology designed for ultra-low-power communication. Suitable for simple IoT devices with infrequent data transmission.
- **NB-IoT (Narrowband IoT)**: Uses licensed cellular spectrum, providing secure, reliable, and scalable communication. Widely used in smart utilities and infrastructure monitoring.
- **LTE-M (LTE for Machines)**: Provides better mobility and higher bandwidth than NB-IoT, suitable for wearables and connected vehicles.
- **5G**: Enables advanced IoT use cases such as connected cars, smart manufacturing, and immersive augmented reality due to ultra-low latency and high bandwidth.

5.5 IoT STANDARDS AND PROTOCOLS

One of the most critical aspects of Internet of Things (IoT) systems is the need for standardization. Since IoT involves billions of devices from diverse manufacturers, each with different designs and technologies, establishing common standards and protocols is essential. Standardization not only ensures interoperability between devices but also guarantees scalability, reliability, and security of IoT deployments. Without widely accepted standards, IoT ecosystems would remain fragmented, making large-scale implementations such as smart cities impossible to sustain.

5.5.1 Application Layer Protocols

At the application layer, protocols define how IoT devices communicate with end-user applications and services. Several protocols are specifically designed to support lightweight, resource-constrained environments.

The Message Queuing Telemetry Transport (MQTT) protocol is a popular publish–subscribe standard, optimized for low-bandwidth and high-latency networks. It is particularly effective in remote sensing and monitoring applications. The Constrained Application Protocol (CoAP), which runs over UDP, is tailored for constrained devices and supports machine-to-machine (M2M) communication. In enterprise systems, the Advanced Message Queuing Protocol (AMQP) is widely used because of its emphasis on secure and reliable message delivery. Traditional HTTP/HTTPS protocols, although heavier, are still adopted because of their universal acceptance and compatibility with web applications.

5.5.2 Network Layer Protocols

The network layer focuses on addressing, routing, and transmitting IoT data. Given the massive number of devices in IoT, IPv4 addressing is inadequate, leading to the adoption of IPv6, which provides a vastly expanded address space. However, IPv6 alone is not sufficient for resource-constrained networks. Protocols such as 6LoWPAN (IPv6 over Low-power Wireless Personal Area Networks) make IPv6 compatible with lightweight devices. Additionally, the Routing Protocol for Low-Power and Lossy Networks (RPL) addresses the unique needs of IoT environments, such as limited power, memory, and unreliable communication channels.

5.5.3 Data Link Layer Protocols

The data link layer provides the physical connectivity and medium access control for IoT devices. Standards such as IEEE 802.15.4 form the basis for low-power wireless technologies including Zigbee. Bluetooth Low Energy (BLE) enables efficient short-range communication, particularly in wearable and healthcare devices. Wi-Fi, despite its higher power consumption, is widely used in home, office, and public IoT systems because of its high data rate and easy integration with internet infrastructure.

5.5.4 Standardization Bodies

IoT standardization is driven by international organizations. IEEE (Institute of Electrical and Electronics Engineers) defines standards for wireless communication. IETF (Internet Engineering Task Force) develops internet-related protocols including IPv6 and RPL. ITU (International Telecommunication Union) addresses global telecommunication standards. ETSI (European Telecommunications Standards Institute) focuses on cellular IoT such as NB-IoT and LTE-M, while OneM2M creates frameworks for global M2M and IoT interoperability. Together, these bodies ensure that IoT ecosystems can function seamlessly across regions and industries.

5.6 AN IoT STRATEGY FOR SMARTER CITIES

The successful implementation of smart city initiatives requires more than technology—it demands a well-planned IoT strategy. Cities must define a roadmap that integrates IoT solutions into urban infrastructure in a way that is secure, scalable, and citizen-focused.

5.6.1 Vision and Objectives

The first step is establishing a clear vision of what the city seeks to achieve. Objectives may include reducing energy consumption, minimizing traffic congestion, improving waste management, or enhancing public safety. The vision must align with long-term urban development goals and sustainability requirements.

5.6.2 Standards and Interoperability

Once the objectives are set, cities must ensure that solutions are built on interoperable standards. This prevents vendor lock-in and allows integration of devices from multiple suppliers. Common standards and protocols also make future upgrades and expansions easier.

5.6.3 Data-Driven Governance

A central component of smart cities is data-driven decision-making. IoT generates massive amounts of data that can be processed using big data analytics and artificial intelligence to optimize services. For example, predictive analytics can forecast energy demand or traffic congestion, enabling better planning and faster responses.

5.6.4 Citizen Participation

Citizens are at the heart of smart cities. Governments must actively involve them through mobile apps, e-governance portals, and participatory platforms. Engaging residents not only improves adoption but also ensures that services meet real community needs.

5.6.5 Security, Scalability, and Sustainability

Finally, a strong IoT strategy must focus on long-term sustainability. Systems should be designed to handle population growth and increasing numbers of devices. At the same time, cybersecurity measures must protect sensitive data, while energy-efficient technologies ensure that IoT deployments remain environmentally sustainable.

5.7 SMART CITY IoT ARCHITECTURE

A smart city IoT architecture provides the blueprint for integrating diverse IoT devices, networks, platforms, and services into a cohesive ecosystem. This architecture typically consists of multiple layers, each responsible for specific tasks.

5.7.1 Device Layer

The device layer forms the foundation of smart city solutions. It consists of sensors and actuators embedded in infrastructure such as streetlights, traffic signals, parking spaces, energy meters, and environmental monitoring units. These devices collect raw data from the physical environment.

5.7.2 Network Layer

The network layer connects devices to higher-level systems using communication technologies such as Wi-Fi, Zigbee, LoRaWAN, NB-IoT, and 5G. Its role is to ensure reliable transmission of data while addressing scalability and interoperability challenges.

5.7.3 Data Layer

The data layer includes cloud computing platforms, local servers, and edge computing devices. It is responsible for data storage, preprocessing, and analysis. Edge computing is especially valuable for time-sensitive applications like traffic control, as it reduces latency by processing data near the source.

5.7.4 Application Layer

The application layer transforms data into citizen-facing services. Examples include mobile apps showing bus schedules, parking availability, or air quality. It ensures that raw sensor data is converted into actionable insights for end-users.

5.7.5 Security Layer

Security is not a standalone component but a cross-cutting layer spanning the entire architecture. It includes authentication mechanisms, encryption techniques, and intrusion detection systems that protect IoT devices and city infrastructure from cyber threats.

5.8 SMART CITY SECURITY ARCHITECTURE DESIGN AND DEVELOPMENT

Security is a cornerstone of smart cities, as these systems manage critical infrastructure and sensitive citizen data. A robust security architecture ensures confidentiality, integrity, and availability (CIA) of information.

5.8.1 Confidentiality

Confidentiality ensures that sensitive information such as citizen identities, financial transactions, and location data is accessible only to authorized entities. Encryption techniques, secure authentication, and role-based access controls are widely used to maintain confidentiality.

5.8.2 Integrity

Integrity guarantees that data is not altered during transmission. Mechanisms such as cryptographic hashing, digital signatures, and blockchain-based systems are employed to preserve data authenticity and prevent tampering.

5.8.3 Availability

Availability ensures that smart city services remain accessible despite cyberattacks, technical failures, or natural disasters. This is achieved by designing redundant systems, distributed architectures, and disaster recovery mechanisms.

5.8.4 Security Mechanisms

To reinforce overall resilience, cities adopt identity and access management systems, secure communication protocols like TLS, DTLS, and IPSec, and continuous monitoring tools for real-time anomaly detection. Additionally, a well-defined incident response strategy ensures that security breaches are handled swiftly and effectively.

5.9 SMART CITY USE-CASE EXAMPLES

5.9.1 Connected Street Lighting

Connected street lighting demonstrates how IoT can improve both energy efficiency and public safety. Smart LED lamps equipped with sensors can adjust brightness based on pedestrian or vehicle movement. They can also be remotely monitored and controlled, reducing maintenance costs. By lowering energy consumption and carbon emissions, connected street lighting contributes significantly to sustainability goals.

5.9.2 Smart Traffic Control

Smart traffic systems address one of the most pressing urban challenges—traffic congestion. IoT-enabled sensors and cameras monitor traffic flow in real time, while AI algorithms dynamically adjust signal timings. These systems reduce waiting times, fuel usage, and emissions. Emergency vehicles receive priority access, improving response times. Integration with parking systems guides drivers to available spaces, further enhancing mobility.

5.9.3 Connected Environment

Environmental sustainability is a central objective of smart cities. IoT-based environmental monitoring systems use sensors to track air quality, noise levels, and water purity across urban areas. Data is analyzed to detect pollution hotspots and predict risks. For example, real-time air quality alerts can inform citizens about health hazards, while smart water management systems detect leaks to minimize wastage and optimize usage.

◆◆◆